THE INCOME STREAM
A Simplified Guide to
Real Estate Investment Analysis

by Robert M Goodman

ons
and, TX 78597

WARNING - DISCLAIMER

The information and procedures contained in this book are based upon the research and the personal and professional experience of the author. They are not intended as a substitute for consulting with your personal attorney, CPA, or any other professionals. The publishers and author are not responsible for any adverse consequences caused, or alleged to be caused, directly or indirectly by the information contained in this book. The purposes of this book is to educate, entertain and to provide information in regard to the subject matter covered. If you do not wish to be bound by the above, you may return this book with sales slip to the publisher for a full refund.

Published by:
Brookstone Publications
3100 Padre Blvd
South Padre Island, TX 78597

Library of Congress Catalog Number   98-72253

ISBN: 0-9664474-7-6

Printed in the United States of America

10 9 8 7 6 5 4 3 2 1

ABOUT THE AUTHOR

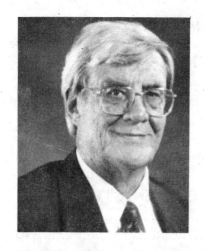

Bob Goodman brings much experience to the income stream, having real estate experience spanning more than 38 years. His career began with his uncle Thomas W. Goodman of Virginia who as a builder / developer became his mentor and guide.

Bob's vast real estate career includes his work as the developer and general partner in the development and management of 21 major apartment and office complexes throughout the southeast, with one high-rise building.

He also has put together 15 real estate investment syndications owning and managing apartment complexes, motels and office buildings throughout the southeast. In these endeavors, with Bob as its President and CEO, his company acted as syndicator and general partner.

Bob Goodman has presented hundreds of real estate investment seminars to the public. He was also an instructor of syndications for the National Association of Realtors. He has also served as Executive Vice President of a Real Estate Investment Trust.

He is currently president and CEO of a real estate company as a Coldwell Banker franchisee in a south Texas resort city. In addition, his current company handles real estate sales, resort rentals, property management and real estate investment counseling.

THE INCOME STREAM
"A SIMPLIFIED GUIDE TO REAL ESTATE INVESTMENT ANALYSIS"

TABLE OF CONTENTS

Page

CHAPTER 1 - THE INCOME STREAM - JUGULAR VEIN OF AN
             INVESTMENT 1
    What about Location? 2
    What is the Income Stream? 4
    The Landlord and the Tenant 5
    Quality and Durability of the Income Stream 9

CHAPTER 2 - IDENTIFYING THE "YIELD ELEMENTS" OF THE
             INCOME STREAM 15
    The "Cash" Yield 16
    The "Tax Shelter" Yield 16
    Taxed Deferred Exchange 19
    The "Equity Build-Up" Yield 21
    The "Appreciation" Yield 21
    How Inflation Affects Values 22
    Horn of Plenty 24
    When the Yields are Available 27
    Summarizing the Four Yields 28

CHAPTER 3 - IDENTIFYING THE INCOME STREAM ON THE
             APOD WORKSHEET 30
    Explaining the Annual Property Operating Data Form 31
    Uses of the APOD Form 33
    Value Established by Power to Produce 35
    Beginning of Sample Property 38

CHAPTER 4 - IDENTIFYING THE INCOME STREAM ON THE
             CFA WORKSHEET 44
    Explaining the Cash Flow Analysis Worksheet 46
    The Growth Factor 54

CHAPTER 5 - IDENTIFYING THE INCOME STREAM ON THE ACS WORKSHEET 58

Calculations of Sales Proceeds 61

Looking at the ACS Line by Line 64

CHAPTER 6 - INTRO TO THE INTERNAL RATE OF RETURN 69

Understanding Rules of Thumb 70

The Capitalization Rate 76

IRR Introduced 77

Discounted Cash Flow - What is it? 79

Concept of Time Value of Money 79

Net Present Value - What is it? 81

CHAPTER 7 - THE INTERNAL RATE OF RETURN 83

The "Tee Bar" 83

Bringing The Combined Yields Into One Rate of Return ... 86

How to Combine Yield to One Rate of Return 86

The Installment Loan Pattern and the Investment
Pattern 89

The IRR Defined 95

Calculators of the IRR 97

CHAPTER 8 - VALUING THE REAL ESTATE USING THE INCOME STREAM 98

Valuing the Property Using the NOI 99

How to Arrive at a Value to Suit Your Personal IRR 102

Valuing the Property Using the IRR 103

The Over-Priced Property 105

CHAPTER 9 - THE "VARIABLES" OF INVESTMENT ANALYSIS, LIQUIDITY AND RISK 108

Let's Talk About Liquidity 108

Let's Talk About Risk 110

The Investment Variables 113

The Investment Variables and Locating Them on the
Offering Documents 115

Value Predicated on the Future 114

CHAPTER 10 - THE INVESTMENT CURVES AND THE COMPUTER 125
When to Sell, Exchange, or Refinance 125
Different People - Different Value, Same Property 127
The Investment Alternatives 134
The Investment Base Concept 137
Introducing the FMRR 138
A Look at the Computer 140

CHAPTER 11 - OWNERSHIP & MANAGEMENT OF INVESTMENT REAL ESTATE 152
The Power of Leverage 153
How to Identify a Debt Coverage Ratio 156
Management of Your Investments 156
Management Mistakes Owners Make 157
"The Greater Fool" 158
The Second Most Important Consideration 159

CHAPTER 12 - HOW TO ANALYZE YIELDS FROM OTHER INVESTMENT FORMS 162
Alternative Investment Comparisons 163
"The Significant Six" 164
A Look at Gold, Stocks, Mortgages, Land & Bonds 166
Savings Accounts, and Life Insurance 172
Conclusion 176

APPENDIX A - BLANK FORMS 177

APPENDIX B - REA/L ESTATE SOFTWARE INFORMATION 182

ACKNOWLEDGMENTS

This book has been many years in the making. It was created after hundreds of sessions designed to help others to understand the subject, failed. At least, on a long term basis. Attendees received, enjoyed and sincerely appreciated the information, however, without a reference the techniques became quickly lost. This prompted The Income Stream.

First thanks needs to go to my first born, Thomas W Goodman II, for his major contribution. He is highly trained in this subject and practices daily. His help and encouragement are deeply appreciated. Thanks to those good friends and associates who reviewed this material and provided many helpful suggestions.

Sincere appreciation to Wanda Vice, a great lady and wonderful helper. To Linda Webster, Indexer, Austin, Texas. Mercedes Printing of Mercedes, Texas, and to Quantum Designs of Provo, Utah.

Bob Goodman

INTRODUCTION

The Income Stream is written and designed to help you know how to select and evaluate good real estate investments. It is presented in a serious, yet simple no-nonsense, easy to grasp manner. It will give you a beginning understanding of the techniques of investment evaluation used by the pros.

This is not a real estate technical manual filled with elaborate theories and formulas. This is not a book on "How to Get Rich in Real Estate". Rather, it will help you to understand the analysis process. The "Get Rich in Real Estate" part will take care of itself.

The Income Stream takes you beyond the 'thumb-rules' and 'quick-multipliers' to the solid techniques used today by successful real estate investors. After giving you a clear, concise understanding of the valuation process, it teaches you; (1) how to find a good potential investment, (2) how to understand and uncover its real yields and (3) how to value them. It will also give you a broad understanding of how to deal with risk.

The Income Stream will prepare you to enter, with a

I

giant leap forward, the world of real estate investing. Enjoyed previously by only the few, you may have this advantage if you will take the time to know. Thanks to the computer and modern techniques, this process has become relatively easy.

The Income Stream will also help you to develop your philosophy of investing and give you a foundation of understanding that will help you in all phases of your financial activity.

To help you attain your share of **The Income Stream** let's begin by taking a quick look at the superior characteristics of real estate over other types of investments. Here are the real advantages:

1- BETTER YIELDS

With all things considered Real Estate has categorically produced better, higher yields than any other investment options.

2- HIGH LEVERAGE POTENTIAL (MORTGAGEABLE)

Real Estate, because it is fixed and unique it enjoys the distinction of being the most

II

mortgageable of all investments. As we go on you will see the great value of this.

3-   TAX SHELTER

To encourage economic growth and development the Federal Government offers a favorable tax advantage to those who invest in real estate. These advantages are found in tax deductible depreciation allowances for buildings, even though the building will probably be growing in value. This valuable advantage, along with deductions for mortgage interest, can mean extra income not available with any other investment.

4-   INFLATIONARY HEDGE

Many investments will claim to have some ability to 'hedge' against inflation but real estate far and away is the most valuable and consistent of all inflationary hedges.

5-   EXCHANGEABLE

To further encourage real estate development

the Federal Government will allow you to exchange your investment property for other investment property of the same or higher value without paying any capital gains taxes. It is possible to continue this process until death, and then with a properly constructed will, pass the property on to heirs with a minimum of tax. This is an important segment of estate building and is an extremely valuable advantage. As the investment matures and equities grow, the property must eventually be sold to maintain the highest efficiency from the invested dollar. This is called Pyramiding of Wealth.

If you've been investing in other things for any length of time you can appreciate these valuable qualities.

So, if you are ready to get started let's go for it.... The first thing you will notice is that **The Income Stream** comes with a strong serious emphasis on INCOME.

You shall see this as we move forward.

CHAPTER 1

THE INCOME STREAM

Jugular Vein of an Investment

There is little question that real estate is the greatest single source of wealth among all the investment types. Unless, of course, you were one of Bill Gates original partners or are now investing on the cutting edge of our spectacular new technology. But how many of us have that opportunity? Right, not many.

Real estate is always there. Under all this great wealth and progress of humankind is the land. Yes, the land reaching like a cone to the center of the earth, finite, immovable, limited in supply, sought after and valued by the needs of the ever increasing masses.

Will Rogers had it right when he gave this formula for getting rich "FIND OUT WHERE THE PEOPLE ARE GOING - GET THERE FIRST AND BUY THE LAND".

Each time a new baby is spanked into life a need is created. A need for more space, more homes, more schools, more stores, offices, factories . . .More of everything. The NEED IS ENDLESS.

To help direct you to your share and to give you a greater understanding we have created THE INCOME STREAM. In order to provide you with the right mind set we ask you to remember what a famous football coach said to his team "WINNING ISN'T EVERYTHING - IT'S THE ONLY THING".

Considering your hard earned dollars . . .INCOME IS THE ONLY THING when investing in real estate, as you shall see.

WHAT ABOUT LOCATION?.

If someone were to ask you to recite the three most im-portant characteristics of a real estate investment you would most probably reply, **"LOCATION! LOCATION! LOCATION!"**.

This well known cliche is fun to say because it is startling by its redundancy and easy to visualize. It sounds good because it suddenly conjures up all the great locations that others own and you wish you had. However, buying only for "location, location, location" is, in fact, very **elementary and short-sighted.** It embraces only a small segment of what one really should look for in a real estate investment. Certainly, it is far from the most important thing to be considered. Here's why.

Following this popular advice, suppose you did buy "location, location, location". After you have enjoyed the prestige of ownership of this notorious property for a while, you begin to notice **your investment yield is very poor.** You suddenly realize that you paid too much for the property or that the present building is not at its highest and best use. As you count your losses, you now realize that there is another consideration which is much more critical than "location, location, location', namely, "The Income Stream" of the investment, the money that this 'investment' was supposed to provide. This then becomes the most important investment consideration of all. You are investing to make money, aren't you? Then, keep your eye on the income stream and all the elements that affect it. The income stream is the lifeline, the jugular vein of the investment.

WHAT IS THE INCOME STREAM?

The Income Stream is the total of all the financial benefits derived from ownership of a property. As a stream of water has many tributaries, so also does an investment real estate property have many contributing elements. Together these elements constitute the "Main Stream" of income which we call "The Income Stream". It is our purpose to show the reader how to locate and examine each of these tributaries, then to bring them down to one common unit of income from which a single yield rate and value can be derived.

LOCATION IS IMPORTANT.

Before you are left with the impression that location is not important, consider this example. A nine-story office building located in a small town would obviously have more value than an identical nine-story office building located in the middle of the Sahara Desert. This is simply because there are fewer people in the desert to rent it.

It is equally obvious that the same nine-story office building located on the corner of 18th and Pennsylvania Avenue, NW, Washington, D.C. just two blocks from the White House, would have a greater value than that located in a small town. Same building, just different locations, locations where there are higher concentrations of people demanding facilities of this sort. Where the demand is high the rents are high. This translates into higher property values because of location. Yes. But aren't we really talking about the money, the yield, the "Income Stream?" Of course we are. Certainly, location is important , but only as it enhances the "Income Stream."

THE LANDLORD AND THE TENANT

Location is of ultimate importance to you if you are a "user". Just as the Income Stream is of ultimate importance to you if you are an "investor". The user's, or the tenant's point of view is entirely different from that of an investor. A seller of automobiles, hamburgers, or gasoline (the property user) must depend upon his location to provide the traffic necessary to sustain his business. Some may argue, "Well, the greater the volume of business the higher the rents". This is not necessarily so. While location is a great contributor to successful business generation it is still only a contributor. There are many other factors that serve to make up a successful business, none of which are connected to the real estate. A skillfully prepared lease can give the landlord some of these benefits -- which we call rent over-rides -- but business risks and business profits belong to the user, not the landlord.

THE BUSINESS AND THE REAL ESTATE VIEWED SEPARATELY

If the investor is both the user and the landlord of the same property, the two income sources should be separated and analyzed individually. When the primary business of the investment is that of renting space, the income should be attributed to the Real Estate. When the income is from the business, it should be attributed to the business.

Some Examples of 'Space for Rent':

Self-storage Units
Homes/Apartments/Duplexes
Mobile Home/ R-V Spaces
Shopping Centers
Office Space
Warehouse Space
Hotel/Motel Space
Parking Lots and Garages
Commercial Stores

These are examples where space is the main commodity. It can and should be considered a real estate investment. There are many others. An analysis of its value should be made on the basis of its earning power alone.

The income stream from an Eastern Oriental Belly Dancing School cannot be counted toward the value of the building in which it operates, even though the property may be owned by the school operator. This is because the major function of the business is not to rent space but rather to teach belly dancing. The business profits belong to the business, the profits from space rented belong to the property.

An income property should be judged on its ability to produce income. All other characteristics or amenities are important only as they enhance and strengthen the INCOME STREAM.

This should be a cardinal rule for all real estate investors!

BEWARE OF SMOKE SCREENS

All too often investment property will be presented to a buyer with great emphasis on its replacement value, saying, "Buy this building because you cannot replace it at today's construction cost". Yet the property is probably unrentable at the "market rates" for some undefined reason, thereby making what appears to be a bargain, not a bargain at all. Another may say, "This is a good investment because the rents are low and can be increased". In reality the rents may be low as a result of some deficiency, such as lack of parking, poor access, deferred maintenance or functional obsolescence, thus, making a rental increase impossible.

These and other "smoke screens" tend to cloud the issue

of the income stream. Remember, when you buy an investment you do so anticipating a return. Your prime objective is to safeguard your principal and make a return. To do this you must push past the "smoke screens" and go directly to the heart of the matter. Examine the Income Stream. If you don't, it might not be so easy to get that next buyer. You may find your property hard to sell. It may require a price reduction below cost in order to liquidate.

Any knowledgeable broker will tell you that the properties with the greatest liquidity problems are those that are overpriced, either through unrealistic desires of the owner or a poor purchase in the first place. The income stream simply does not justify the selling price. On the other hand, good properties with clearly defined income streams will sell more quickly if a reasonable return for risk is offered. With the importance of the Income Stream explained, let's go to the heart of it.

TEST THE INCOME STREAM

Before we analyze and evaluate the Income Stream, let's

explore the caliber of the income source from several perspectives. The strength of the Income Stream must be tested to determine its value. This is done by examining "Quantity, Quality and Durability." You may compare this examination to taking the pulse, blood pressure and temperature of a patient. The vital signs of an investment are its Quantity, Quality and Durability.

TESTING THE "QUANTITY" OF INCOME

Quantity is the amount of income the stream produces. In succeeding chapters we will demonstrate how to identify, evaluate and consolidate the elements (the tributaries) that constitute the Income Stream. We will then show you how to arrive at the "Quantity" factor in a clear, concise way.

TESTING THE "QUALITY" OF INCOME

Quality of income has to do with the caliber of the credit behind the Income Stream. This is highly judgmental by the owner/investor but one that must be made. In order to determine this "caliber of credit", one must determine who is responsible for rents. One must also be aware of the credit worthiness and financial standing of the renting company or individual. In order to know this, you must examine the credit report and financial statement of the tenant. This activity is of supreme importance because it reveals the "Quality" of the Income Stream. What is the value of a high rent (Quantity) or long lease (Durability) if you can't collect on it? At one end, the "Quality" spectrum may contain "Jobless Joe Flyer" and his common law wife as tenants, who have very poor credit and no assets, at the other end is AT&T or General Motors. Somewhere between these two extremes lies the "Quality" factor. At one end of the spectrum the risk is very high, at the other end it is very low. An evaluation of the "Quality" of the Income Stream then is a judgmental matter and must be made by the owner/investor. The financial credit strength or weakness of the tenant constitutes part of the risk and must be reflected in the rents charged.

TESTING THE "DURABILITY" OF INCOME

Durability has to do with the **length** and **stability** of the Income Stream, particularly as it is affected by the contract conditions found in the lease or rental agreement.

A landlord, who had a rent escalating, 30-year-net lease with AT&T (which on the surface, is one of the best leases you can get) would not really have much if AT&T had a "contract condition" in the lease which said they could move out in 60 days. This would be an example of good quality but poor durability.

What is good "Durability" as opposed to poor "Durability "? The "Durability" spectrum could have a "no notice move out" clause at one end, and a "rent escalating, net, long term lease, with no back-doors or escape clauses" at the other. Again, somewhere between the two lies the real "Durability" factor of the investment. This is another part of the factor that makes up the risk and must be examined carefully by the prospective investor.

BEST OF ALL WORLDS NOT AVAILABLE

It is not reasonable to expect that all three elements - Quantity, Quality and Durability will be present in their highest forms in any single investment lease. It is obvious that investment leases of high "Quality" and great "Durability" will not have the best "Quantity" simply because these investment leases are much in demand and can go at a lower rental rate.

Example: Almost all investors would like to have a long term, rent escalating, lease with Sears, Roebuck & Co. because of Sears' excellent credit rating. However, Sears understands this demand for their leases and can therefore drive a better bargain as far as "Quantity" goes.

Some investors are willing to take less quantity of income in exchange for a reduced risk created by good quality and durability of income. On the other hand, some investors may be willing to take less Quality or Durability in order to receive more Quantity as illustrated in Figure 1. It's sort of like a triangle. If we move toward one income characteristic, we move away from the other two. An investor needs to find his own risk and comfort level and charge a commensurate rental rate to justify the reduction of the other two qualities.

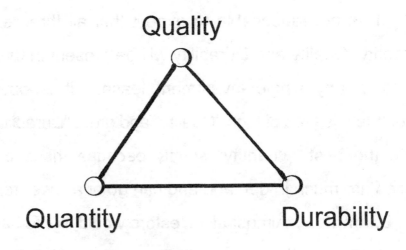

EXHIBIT NO. 1

SUMMARY

An income property should be judged by its ability to produce income. All other amenities are important only as they enhance and strengthen the Income Stream. The strength of the Income Stream must be tested to determine its real value by an examination of the Quantity, Quality and Durability of the stream itself.

On our way to determining the Quantity of income we will next show how to IDENTIFY AND VALUATE the Income Stream. To the serious investor or student of investment, this process will prove exciting and extremely useful.

CHAPTER 2

IDENTIFYING THE "YIELD ELEMENTS"
OF THE INCOME STREAM

There are four basic yields from ownership of investment real estate. These are in effect the tributaries of the Income Stream. They are all inclusive, there are no others. Not all four characteristics are found in all real estate investments. Some will contain part of them, other investments may contain them all. In fact most of them will. But in every real estate investment at least one of the characteristics will be present. Learn these four simple yields, identify their sources, learn to value them and you have removed a great portion of the mystery surrounding real estate investing. Gaining an understanding of these four yields and how they work can also help reduce a portion of the so-called risk.

The four yields are:
1. CASH
2. TAX SHELTER
3. EQUITY BUILD-UP
4. APPRECIATION

THE CASH YIELD #1

There is hardly anyone who does not understand what cash is and its power to purchase. However, in the Real Estate sense Cash is defined as "the money left over after vacancies, operating expenses and mortgage payments", but before income taxes. There are certainly no mysteries here.

THE "TAX SHELTER" YIELD #2

The "Tax Shelter" Yield is the same as the "Cash Yield" except that it is calculated AFTER the income tax consequences.

In an effort to encourage economic growth through real estate development, the Federal Government allows the depreciation of buildings even though they may be, and probably are, increasing in value. (Let the reader understand that depreciation allowed by the IRS, now called COST RECOVERY, and actual deterioration of buildings are in no way related.) Some people view depreciation as an actual "return of capital" or a recapture of their money invested. Hence the new name COST RECOVERY. This is an acceptable viewpoint even though when the building is sold the buyers equity will, more than likely, be returned. Exceptions might be some major functional obsolescence, deferred maintenance, or a serious drop in the market value, again. The IRS takes the view that a depreciation allowance is available for every new owner, regardless of how much the previous owner depreciated the building. Depreciation from here forward will be called COST RECOVERY. This cost recovery allowance, when coupled with the "interest paid on mortgages" deduction and "cost recovery allowance" for personal property, becomes a shelter for the income from the property that would otherwise be taxable. This is called "tax shelter".

In well leveraged, properly structured, real estate investments it is entirely possible to shelter not only the income derived from the investment itself but also to have excess tax shelter to apply against income derived from other investment sources. Therefore, "Tax Shelter" can be, and often is a "hard-dollar" cash yield.

When this excess tax shelter is applied to other income it will provide a cash yield. It comes from tax savings on income earned outside the investment itself, i.e. one's other investments or business.

Since this cash yield comes from your ownership of depreciated property, it should be attributed to the property and counted as part of its yield. This is called the "Tax Shelter" yield.

It is important to note here that these "Tax Shelter" yields are usually best available during the early years of ownership, depending upon the type of depreciation schedule selected. Also, as the investment matures and mortgages are reduced, less money is paid toward interest. Therefore, this portion of the

Income Stream will be declining. We will see more clearly how this works in examples shown in later chapters. The investor must carefully note where and when these downward trends (investment curves) take place (See Chapter 10).

When these curves do occur and the "yield to equity" ratio takes a downward trend, and it surely will, the investor can consider another tremendously advantageous "tax shelter" called the Tax Deferred Exchange. Let's take a small sidestep for just a moment and talk about the tax-deferred exchange.

TAX-DEFERRED EXCHANGE

To further encourage real estate development, the Federal Government has established a device called a "Tax Deferred" exchange. In it the IRS will allow you to "Exchange" your investment property for another investment property of the same or higher value without requiring the payment of any tax on any earned capital gains. This tax is deferred and can continue to be deferred by subsequent tax deferred exchanges as long as you like until a final sale is made. With the use of this investment tool it is possible to exchange, say, an apartment complex for a shopping center, an office complex for some land or any combination of these for any one of the many real estate investment types. The rules state that an exchange must be made "like for like". The "like" being a real estate investment. Remember, though, in order to achieve the tax deferred status, an exchange must be made for a property of equal or greater value.

With your new building acquired through a "Tax Deferred Exchange" you can start the tax shelter all over again, from depreciation (cost recovery), etc. However, your old tax basis will be carried forward into the new property. Because tax laws are continually changing and the Tax Deferred Exchange is a highly technical activity, A CPA, a tax lawyer, or one of the professional groups who specialize in #1031 tax-free exchanges must always be consulted when considering using its advantages. This is, by the way, the main ingredient for The Pyramiding of Wealth through Real Estate.

THE "EQUITY BUILD-UP" YIELD #3

Equity build-up, the third tributary of the Income Stream, is the increase in equity ownership of the property gained by the paying down of the mortgage.

Some may say that, "this is not a yield because I am, in effect, paying the mortgage down from my income from the property". This, however, is not true in a pure investment sense. Cash yields from real estate investments are always computed after vacancies, operating expenses and mortgage payments have been subtracted from the gross income. (See definition of "CASH YIELD" on page 16) The tenants, then, actually make the mortgage payments. The income derived, or the equity built up therefrom is counted as a part of your yield from ownership of the property.

THE "APPRECIATION" YIELD #4

Appreciation is, for the most part, income derived from an increase in value created by forces outside of the original investment itself. Some of these external forces are: shifts in the demands of people, inflation, and other general economic conditions. It may also occur when you upgrade and otherwise enhance the property.

DEMANDS OF PEOPLE AFFECT THE APPRECIATION YIELD

How does this work? People make value. Without the needs and demands of people, there would be no value. The largest diamond ever found would be of no value to the only man left on earth. Ten million bushels of wheat are of no value to the last man on earth. People, indeed, make value. As their demands go up, so does the use of real property. The intensity of use then translates itself into higher rents, therefore, higher value.

HOW INFLATION AFFECTS VALUES

Appreciation of value through inflation can be illustrated as follows:

As the costs of new buildings rise, that is, as the current cost of labor, bricks, lumber and concrete required to build new buildings increase, the value of existing buildings (or the labor, bricks, lumber and concrete used to replace them) will rise also. Of course, there needs to be a discounting of value of older existing property to allow for deterioration and obsolescence.

Nevertheless, the value of existing buildings do tend to rise to coincide with their replacement value as long as the demand for their use persists.

Yield from "Appreciation" is a significant investment factor and has been a major source to make people rich. Probably the greatest single source of wealth for the vast majority of Americans today is their personal residence. Homes that have grown tremendously in value throughout years of double digit inflation are the cause of this wealth.

Question: Would you sell a house that you bought ten years ago for the price you paid for it? Of course you would not, but you get the point.

APPRECIATION AND UPKEEP

"Appreciation" of value is also achieved through the increase in desirability of a property. This desirability is brought on by good management, good upkeep and a unique location. Often "run-down" properties are purchased, up-graded and sold at tremendous profits. This is the basic secret for success contained in most "Make a Fortune in Real Estate" type books. It illustrates for us again the importance of the "Appreciation" yield of our Income Stream.

THE HORN OF PLENTY

To graphically illustrate the affects of Yield #3: The Equity Build-up Yield; and Yield #4: The Appreciation Yield; here's an example. Let's suppose that you buy a duplex for $100,000. You take out an 80% mortgage and put down 20%.

Using a Time & Money scale it would look like this:

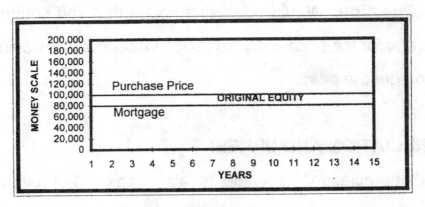

EXHIBIT NO. 2

As the investment moves along in time we notice that the prices of similar properties are going up and we are able to raise our rents. Remember that the value is established according to income. Therefore as our rents rise, our total value moves up commensurately.

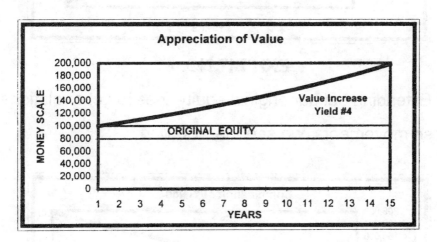

EXHIBIT NO. 3

During this period, as we move along the time line, we have been making our mortgage payments. We also notice that our mortgage balance is declining.

Graphically it could look like this:

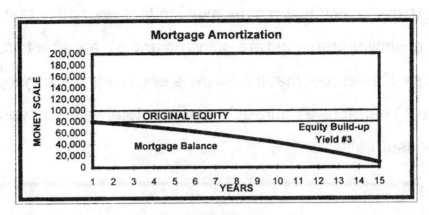

EXHIBIT NO. 4

Extending out our original equity lines to get a relationship to these movements, we see the following:

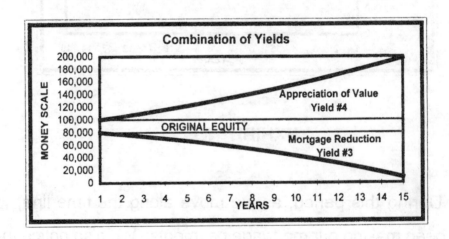

EXHIBIT NO. 5

Here you can instantly see the significant impact of Yield #3 and #4. We (laughingly) call this the Horn of Plenty.

WHEN ARE THE YIELDS AVAILABLE?

Yields #I and #2, Cash and Tax Shelter, are considered to be NOW yields in that they may start to be enjoyed within the first 12 months of ownership. Yields 3 and 4, Equity Build-up and Appreciation, are to be enjoyed later. Yield 3, the Equity Build-up Yield, must await a sale or it can be had earlier upon the instance of a refinance. Yields from a refinance are usually free from income tax. Yield 4, the Appreciation Yield, can be had only upon the sale or exchange of the property.

ONE MORE WORD ABOUT APPRECIATION

We tend to ignore the powerful contribution of APPRECIATION. On the surface, its benefits may appear remote in that they occur some time in the distant future and at a seemingly undeterminable rate. Yet fabulous fortunes are made in land speculation using *value appreciation* as its only source. It is certainly not to be ignored or considered lightly. As we get further into the valuation phase you will begin to see the power of this yield form.

SUMMARIZING THE 4 YIELDS WHICH MAKE UP THE INCOME STREAM

There are four separate and distinct yields to investment real estate. To analyze a property for its real value <u>all four must be considered</u>. To overlook one or two could mean that you are missing 50 to 75% of the potential income. Or, you could easily "by-pass" a good investment. On the other hand, you could buy a poor investment that looked good only on the surface.

Learn these four yields as you know the names of your children. A knowledge of them is extremely important. We will use them throughout our income stream "identification" and "valuation" sections.

Again, they are:

1. CASH =   Income remaining, after vacancy, expenses and mortgage payments and before income taxes.

2. TAX SHELTER =   Income derived by sheltering the cash yields from Income Taxes and also as applied to other

income from different sources.

3. EQUITY BUILD-UP = Income derived from equity gained through paying down the mortgage.

4. APPRECIATION = Income gained through increase in value created by increased rents and inflation.

CHAPTER 3
IDENTIFYING THE INCOME STREAM ON THE APOD

Up to this point we have established that the first and most important investment criterion is "The Income Stream". We have discussed the necessity of an internal examination of the income stream by a review of its Quantity, Quality and Durability. We have also identified the four elements that make up the income stream. Our next efforts will go to identify the four yields of the income stream on the investment offering documents.

To do so we will use the three major analysis forms

currently being used by the National Association of Realtors (NAR). More specifically the Commercial Investment Real Estate Institute of the NAR, which has granted special permission for their use here. These forms are the:

1. Annual Property Operating Data Worksheet (APOD)
2. Cash Flow Analysis Worksheet (CFA)
3. Alternative Cash Sale Worksheet (ACS)

There are many good forms available, some with even greater detail. However, because of their broad usage we have elected to use these particular forms as a standard. As you have properties presented to you by knowledgeable brokers, these forms will most likely be those used.

EXPLAINING THE ANNUAL PROPERTY OPERATING DATA FORM

At this point in our search for the Income Stream, it is important that you become familiar with the APOD worksheet (Annual Property Operating Data Form, Exhibit No. 6).

Annual Property Operating Data

Name _____

Location _____

Type of Property _____   Purchase Price _____

Size of Property _____ (Sq. Ft./Units)   Acquisition Costs _____

Loan Points _____

Purpose _____   Down Payment _____

Assessed/Appraised Values			Existing	Balance	Payment	#Pmts. /Yr.	nterest	Term
Land	_____	_____	1st	_____	_____	_____	_____	_____
Improvements	_____	_____	2nd	_____	_____	_____	_____	_____
Personal Property	_____							
Total	_____	100%	Potential					
			1st	_____	_____	_____	_____	_____
Adjusted Basis as of:	_____		2nd	_____	_____	_____	_____	_____

	ALL FIGURES ARE ANNUAL	$/SQ FT or $/Unit	% of GOI		COMMENTS/FOOTNOTES
1	POTENTIAL RENTAL INCOME	_____		_____	_____
2	Plus: Other Income (affected by vacancy)			_____	_____
3	Less: Vacancy & Cr. Losses	(_____	_____)	_____	_____
4	EFFECTIVE RENTAL INCOME			_____	_____
5	Plus: Other Income (not affected by vacancy)			_____	_____
6	GROSS OPERATING INCOME	_____		_____	_____
	OPERATING EXPENSES:				
7	Real Estate Taxes	_____	_____	_____	_____
8	Personal Property Taxes	_____	_____	_____	_____
9	Property Insurance	_____	_____	_____	_____
10	Off Site Management	_____	_____	_____	_____
11	Payroll	_____	_____	_____	_____
12	Expenses/Benefits	_____	_____	_____	_____
13	Taxes/Worker's Compensation	_____	_____	_____	_____
14	Repairs and Maintenance	_____	_____	_____	_____
	Utilities:				
15	_____	_____	_____	_____	_____
16	_____	_____	_____	_____	_____
17	_____	_____	_____	_____	_____
18	_____	_____	_____	_____	_____
19	Accounting and Legal	_____	_____	_____	_____
20	Licenses/Permits	_____	_____	_____	_____
21	Advertising	_____	_____	_____	_____
22	Supplies	_____	_____	_____	_____
23	Miscellaneous Contract Services:				_____
24	_____	_____	_____	_____	_____
25	_____	_____	_____	_____	_____
26	_____	_____	_____	_____	_____
27	_____	_____	_____	_____	_____
28	_____	_____	_____	_____	_____
29	TOTAL OPERATING EXPENSES	_____	_____	_____	_____
30	NET OPERATING INCOME	_____	_____	_____	_____
31	Less: Annual Debt Service	_____	_____	_____	_____
32	Less: Funded Reserves	_____	_____	_____	_____
33	Less: Leasing Commissions	_____	_____	_____	_____
34	Less: Capital Additions	_____	_____	_____	_____
35	CASH FLOW BEFORE TAXES	_____	_____	_____	_____

The statements and figures herein, while not guaranteed, are secured from sources we believe authoritative.   Prepared by: _____

EXHIBIT NO. 6
Page 32

Take a moment to study its contents. Effectively, the APOD is nothing more than an Income and Expense Operating Statement organized to illustrate the investment dynamics of a real estate investment. Notice that it differs from a strict accounting income and expense statement in that it does not include mortgage interest or depreciation in with the expenses. That will come later. Let's take a detailed look at this form, and insert an example as we go along. Before we go into the form, however, let's examine some of its principal uses.

USES OF THE APOD

The APOD Form has three primary uses:

No. 1 - The Owner's Statement

The first use is to organize information obtained from the current owner of a property under consideration for purchase. When the APOD is used for this purpose, the term "Owner's Statement" should be placed on the line titled, PURPOSE. The information from the owner should then be inserted on the form. In order to have as complete an information package as possible, it is best where practical to fill in ALL items or insert an

N/A to show that that particular item does not apply; also that the information be accurate and verifiable.

No. 2 - The Broker's Reconstruction Statement

The second use of the APOD is to make a comparison of the information received from the owner with the actual market conditions. This should be done by a knowledgeable real estate broker or an experienced investor. Not that the owner would intentionally deceive a buyer; owners just don't do that sort of thing, or do they? Or perhaps he, the owner, might not be in touch with what's happening in the market. It may also be that he has overlooked some item of income or expense. So, with this APOD, you gather information to establish the validity of the numbers being used. For example, the rents currently being charged could be lower than market rents (market rents are the rents paid for comparable properties.) therefore justifying an increase. Or the property insurance could be understated because the property is under-insured. Certain expense items could have been forgotten or omitted. Or a higher tax assessment may be forth coming, etc. Each of these situations could drastically alter the income stream and thereby affect the value. Remember the rule:

THE VALUE OF AN INCOME PROPERTY IS ESTABLISHED ACCORDING TO ITS POWER TO PRODUCE INCOME.

It is important that an investor or broker make this review in order to place the property into a "real world" situation which must be lived with by the new owner. When the form is being used for this purpose, the term "Broker's Reconstructed Statement" should be placed on the "Purpose" line and the updated information inserted.

CAVEAT EMPTOR

When information is inserted that is different from the information given on the Owner's Statement, which is supposed to reflect what the property is doing or could do today, this new information should be made abundantly clear by noting the changes in the column for Comments/Footnotes on the APOD. This new information should also be highly credible and easily verifiable.

No. 3 - The Specific Buyer's Criteria

The third use of the APOD form is to indicate the desires and objectives of a "Specific Buyer". Here are some examples of how buyers may differ: It may be that Buyer 'A' wishes to make a 30% down payment in order to meet his investment objectives. Buyer 'B', on the other hand, may wish to do the maintenance work and perform the property management function himself. Each of these situations would obviously affect the bottom line. When the form is used in this fashion, the term "Specific Buyer" is placed on the Purpose Line and the form filled in to reflect the prospective investor's criteria.

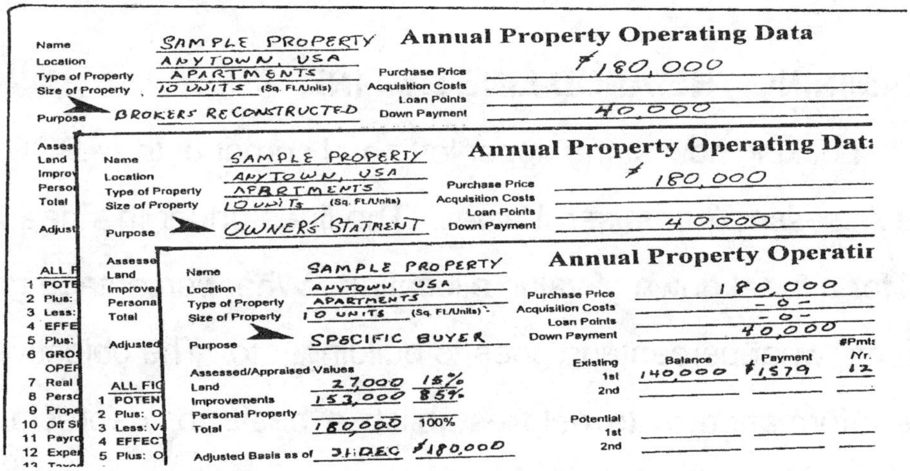
Annual Property Operating Data
Name SAMPLE PROPERTY
Location ANYTOWN, USA
Type of Property APARTMENTS
Size of Property 10 UNITS (Sq. Ft./Units)
Purpose BROKERS RECONSTRUCTED
Purchase Price $180,000
Acquisition Costs
Loan Points
Down Payment 40,000

Annual Property Operating Data
Name SAMPLE PROPERTY
Location ANYTOWN, USA
Type of Property APARTMENTS
Size of Property 10 UNITS (Sq. Ft./Units)
Purpose OWNERS STATMENT
Purchase Price $180,000
Acquisition Costs
Loan Points
Down Payment 40,000

Annual Property Operating Data
Name SAMPLE PROPERTY
Location ANYTOWN, USA
Type of Property APARTMENTS
Size of Property 10 UNITS (Sq. Ft./Units)
Purpose SPECIFIC BUYER
Purchase Price 180,000
Acquisition Costs -0-
Loan Points -0-
Down Payment 40,000
Assessed/Appraised Values
Land 27,000 15%
Improvements 153,000 85%
Personal Property
Total 180,000 100%
Adjusted Basis as of 31-DEC $180,000
Existing Balance Payment #Pmts/Yr.
1st 140,000 $1,579 12
2nd
Potential
1st
2nd

EXHIBIT NO. 7

SIDE NOTES ABOUT THE APOD

The above are a few uses of the APOD. There may be others, though these are the most common. First, it is interesting to note the flexibility of the APOD and secondly the absolute need to cover (and uncover) ALL the elements involved in the investment offering documents so that a clear picture may be seen. A potential buyer should always insist that the documents be complete, accurate and verifiable. All projections and assumptions should be made known. They should be explained and accepted by him, for therein is the bulk of the risk, as we shall see.

EXAMINING THE APOD LINE BY LINE

Looking now at the upper left hand corner of the APOD we see *Assessed/Appraised Values*. The lines under this heading call for a breakdown of value allocation. What percentage goes to land, what percentage goes to building, etc. The objective of this information is to help establish a basis for depreciation which will be needed later on. The usually acceptable sources for this information are the local real estate tax assessor or a qualified appraisal made of the property.

The line titled *Adjusted Basis* is for information to be used when considering the tax implications of ownership and a possible tax-deferred exchange. The tax basis of a newly acquired property is always the same as the purchase price. We will be using this line in our example.

To the right hand side, at the top of the APOD, you will see blanks calling for *Purchase Price*, *Acquisition Costs*, *Loan Costs*, and *Down Payment*. All of these are there to show the buyer what ALL the costs are and the cash required to purchase.

Next is the *Financing* area. This is to show mortgages to be assumed which should be placed under *Existing*. Any new financing, including owner financing, should be placed under *Potential*. This information is straight forward and self-explanatory.

BEGINNING OF SAMPLE PROPERTY

As we go through this segment of "identifying the four investment yields", and throughout the rest of the book, we will use an example of a hypothetical property. Let's suppose you are offered a 10-unit apartment at $180,000 total price with an existing assumable mortgage of $140,000, 13% interest, with a 25-year remaining term. Seller agrees to pay all closing costs. There are no loan points. Rents and expenses have been validated and the APOD is made out to suit your particular investment criteria. Therefore, this APOD use will be titled "Specific Buyer". Filled out using information we have gathered, the APOD would look like this:

Annual Property Operating Data

Name	SAMPLE PROPERTY
Location	ANYTOWN, USA
Type of Property	APARTMENTS
Size of Property	10 UNITS (Sq. Ft./Units)
Purpose	SPECIFIC BUYER

Purchase Price	180,000	
Acquisition Costs	- 0 -	
Loan Points	- 0 -	
Down Payment	40,000	

Assessed/Appraised Values				Existing	Balance	Payment	#Pmts. /Yr.	Interest	Term
Land	27,000	15%		1st	140,000	$1579	12	13%	25y
Improvements	153,000	85%		2nd					
Personal Property									
Total	180,000	100%		Potential					
				1st					
Adjusted Basis as of 31 DEC $180,000				2nd					

ALL FIGURES ARE ANNUAL	$/SQ FT or $/Unit	% of GOI		COMMENTS/FOOTNOTES
1 POTENTIAL RENTAL INCOME			39,120	10 - 1 BR. x 326/mo.
2 Plus: Other Income (affected by vacancy)				
3 Less: Vacancy & Cr. Losses		5% of 39,120)	1,956	
4 EFFECTIVE RENTAL INCOME			37,164	
5 Plus: Other Income (not affected by vacancy)				
6 GROSS OPERATING INCOME			37,164	
OPERATING EXPENSES:				
7 Real Estate Taxes		1,900		
8 Personal Property Taxes				
9 Property Insurance		2,200		
10 Off Site Management				
11 Payroll	0	1,800		
12 Expenses/Benefits				
13 Taxes/Worker's Compensation				
14 Repairs and Maintenance		2,800		
Utilities:				
15 ELECTRICITY	0	1,200		
16 SEWER & WATER	0	1,800		
17 TELEPHONE	0	375		
18				
19 Accounting and Legal	0	425		
20 Licenses/Permits		200		
21 Advertising	0	475		
22 Supplies	0	184		
23 Miscellaneous Contract Services:				
24 JANITORIAL	0	780		
25 LAWN	0	275		
26 RUBBISH	0	675		
27				
28				
29 TOTAL OPERATING EXPENSES	40.7%	15,089		
30 NET OPERATING INCOME		22,075		
31 Less: Annual Debt Service				
32 Less: Funded Reserves				
33 Less: Leasing Commissions				
34 Less: Capital Additions				
35 CASH FLOW BEFORE TAXES		$ 3127		

Prepared by: M. VESTOR

EXHIBIT NO. 8

LET'S NOW GO DOWN THROUGH THE FORM

Lines 1 through 6

These lines deal primarily with the income of the property after subtracting the vacancy and credit losses. It is good practice to put a breakdown of income sources in the "Comments" column or on another page to establish what we call the Rent Roll. The item 'Other Income (affected by vacancy)' could include income from loss of security deposits or any rent subsidy received. The item 'Other Income (not affected by vacancy)' could include income from coin-operated vending machines or other services rendered by the landlord. It is also important for later use that the percentage of vacancy and credit losses be inserted in the percentage (%) column.

Lines 7 through 29

This area is primarily a "Roster of Operating Expenses". It enumerates all of the potential expenses that will be incurred in the operation of the building. The list is an important device, because it helps bring to attention any items that may have been overlooked. It is also important that, for later use, a percentage figure be inserted for Total Operating Expenses.

Lines 30 through 35

The information required here is merely a recapitulation of all of the preceding information. It is also here (lines 33, 34, and 35) that a specific buyer may wish to include and allow for reserves such as appliances, air-conditioning, etc. - also any leasing commissions and anticipated capital additions.

FIRST TRIBUTARY OF THE INCOME STREAM

Well, did you notice that Line 35, *Cash Flow Before Taxes*, is the first of our four yields from Real Estate? This is the first tributary of the Income Stream. This is the *CASH YIELD*.

SUMMARIZING THE APOD

So much for the APOD statement. What you have seen looks pretty straightforward. There are no hidden gimmicks. It is, in effect, an income and expense statement for a property for one year. (All figures on the APOD and CFA worksheets will always be for one year unless otherwise indicated.)

The APOD worksheet by itself, or something similar to it, is more often than not the extent to which most properties are presented to prospective buyers. The APOD is an absolute necessity, but obviously, if our examination of the Income Stream stops there with just the information contained on the APOD worksheet, we have revealed only the *CASH YIELD* and omitted 75% of what the property is all about. We must now go forward to search for the other three income elements:

2- Tax Shelter Income
3- Equity Build-up Income
4- Appreciation Income

To do so we will proceed on to the Cash Flow Analysis Worksheet (CFA) and The Alternative Cash Sales Worksheet (ACS). In doing this we now enter into the world of understanding real estate investing that is enjoyed by very few investors today.

CHAPTER 4

IDENTIFYING THE INCOME STREAM ON THE CFA

Let's now turn to the second form, the Cash Flow Analysis Worksheet (CFA). As we walk through the CFA Form, things appear to get a little more involved. Like anything else, however, if we can cut it up into small pieces -- for good digestion -- it will become crystal clear, abundantly simple and tremendously useful. Before we examine it in detail, one section at a time, let's take a good look at the blank form.

Cash Flow Analysis Worksheet

Property Name			Purchase Price	
Prepared For			Acquisition Costs	
Prepared By			Loan Points	
Date Prepared	8-May-98		Down Payment	

	Mortgage Data			Cost Recovery Data	
	1st Mortgage	2nd Mortgage		Improvements	Personal Property
Amount			Value		
Interest Rate			C. R. Method	SL	
Term			Useful Life		
Payments/Year	12	12	In Service Date		
Periodic Payment	-	-	Recapture		
Annual Debt Service	-	-	(All/None/Excess)		
Comments			Investment Tax Credit ($$ or %)		

Taxable Income

Year:					
1 Potential Rental Income					
2 +Other Income affected by vacancy					
3 -Vacancy & Credit Losses					
4 =Effective Rental Income					
5 +Other Income not affected by vacancy					
6 =Gross Operating Income					
7 -Operating Expenses					
8 =NET OPERATING INCOME					
9 -Interest - 1st Mortgage					
10 -Interest - 2nd Mortgage					
11 -Cost Recovery - Improvements					
12 -Cost Recovery - Personal Property					
13 -					
14 -					
15 =Real Estate Taxable Income					
16 Tax Liability @ (Savings)					

Cash Flows

17 NET OPERATING INCOME (Line 8)					
18 -Annual Debt Service					
19 -					
20 -					
21 =CASH FLOW BEFORE TAXES					
22 -Tax Liability (Savings) (Line 16)					
23 +Investment Tax Credit					
24 =CASH FLOW AFTER TAXES					

EXHIBIT NO. 9

THE CASH FLOW ANALYSIS WORKSHEET LINE BY LINE

Information Blanks at the Top of CFA

The information requested at the top of CFA is the same as the information located at the top of APOD. A simple transfer of information is all that is required.

Mortgage Data

This first section, the Mortgage Data Section, is to display all the mortgages, their terms and conditions. Be sure that all contract provisions such as balloon payments, pay-off penalties or interest variables are noted under 'Comments'.

Cost Recovery Data Section

This information block is to lay out the depreciation (Cost Recovery) method to be used in the analysis. This information is taken directly from the top of the APOD.

Speaking of depreciation, keep in mind that land is not depreciable, only the improvements (buildings) and the personal property (furniture and fixtures). Notice that there is a column for each. This is because personal property may be depreciated at a more rapid rate than the improvements.

NOTE: In order to help insure clarification of the cost allocation to the personal property category, it is helpful that the personal property have a specific price assigned to it in the original property purchase contract or be well documented if purchased for use with the property.

	Mortgage Data			Cost Recovery Data	
	1st Mortgage	2nd Mortgage		Improvements	Personal Property
Amount	140,000		Value	153,000	
Interest Rate	13 %		C. R. Method	SL	
Term	25		Useful Life	27.5	
Payments/Year	12	12	In Service Date	31DEC	
Periodic Payment	1,579		Recapture		
Annual Debt Service	18,948		(All/None/Excess)		
Comments			Investment Tax Credit ($$ or %)		

EXHIBIT NO. 10

The Recapture box is to anticipate a sale of the property which will be noted on the Alternative Cash Sales Worksheet discussed in the next chapter. We will have none in our Sample Property. Investment Tax credits are no longer allowed.

The Taxable Income Section

	Year :	1	T
1 Potential Rental Income		39,120	
2 +Other Income affected by vacancy			
3 -Vacancy & Credit Losses		1,956	
4 =Effective Rental Income		37,164	
5 +Other Income not affected by vacancy			
6 =Gross Operating Income		37,164	
7 -Operating Expenses		15,089	
8 =NET OPERATING INCOME		22,075	
9 -Interest - 1st Mortgage		18,154	
10 -Interest - 2nd Mortgage			
11 -Cost Recovery - Improvements		5,332	
12 -Cost Recovery - Personal Property			
13 -			
14 -			
15 =Real Estate Taxable Income		(1,411)	
16 Tax Liability @ 36 %		(508)	
(Savings)			

EXHIBIT NO. 11

Before we proceed further, turn to page 45 and take a look at lines 1 through 24 on the CFA. Here you will notice a series of five columns attached to them with the word 'year' at the top. From earlier discussions you will recall that, of the four income yields, two of them, the Cash Yield and the Tax Shelter Yield, could be had in the first year; but the other two, the Equity Build-up and the Appreciation Yield, were to be enjoyed only upon the sale of the property, or, in the case of Equity Build-up, at the time of refinance or resale. Therefore, in order to determine what these later yields may be and also show to what extent the income (cash) and deductions (tax shelter) are fluctuating, the CFA form is set up for us to make reasonable projections of the numbers out for a period of five or less years. (Obviously, more columns could be added for a longer projection.)

The Year Line

At the top of each of the five columns, where you see the word Year, insert the date or year number. The major objective of the CFA form is to make reasonable projections into the future in order to display fluctuations in the income stream and to determine what the Appreciation Yield might be.

Lines 1 - 8 of the CFA

The information contained on these lines is taken directly from the APOD worksheet. This is merely a summary of those figures.

Line 9 - 10

Because mortgage interest is deductible from taxable income it is entered here to be subtracted from the Net Operating Income (NOI) for that year.

Lines 11 - 12

Depreciation (Cost Recovery) is also deductible from the Net Operating Income (NOI), therefore, it is entered here. To begin using the CFA and inserting data for our sample property we turn to the top of the sample property APOD statement, here the assessed or appraised values of the property show that 85% of the cost is attributable to the building. Therefore, 85% of $180,000 is $153,000. (We made no allocation for Personal Property.) We then divide $153,000 by the projected 27.5 year life allowable by the Federal Government for apartments to arrive at the annual Cost Recovery, which is $5,564 per year for 27.5 years, except for the first year which is pro-rated because it is not a full year. However, it is close enough for our example.

Inserting "Interest" paid (line 9-10) and the "Cost Recovery" allowance for the year (line 11 - 12) to our form, it will look like this:

	Taxable Income				
Year :	1	2	3	4	5
1 Potential Rental Income	39,120	41,076	43,130	45,286	47,551
2 +Other Income affected by vacancy					
3 -Vacancy & Credit Losses	1,956	2,054	2,156	2,264	2,378
4 =Effective Rental Income	37,164	39,022	40,973	43,022	45,173
5 +Other Income not affected by vacancy					
6 =Gross Operating Income	37,164	39,022	40,973	43,022	45,173
7 -Operating Expenses	15,089	15,843	16,636	17,467	18,341
8 =NET OPERATING INCOME	22,075	23,179	24,338	25,555	26,832
9 -Interest - 1st Mortgage	18,154	18,044	17,920	17,778	17,616
10 -Interest - 2nd Mortgage					
11 -Cost Recovery - Improvements	5,332	5,564	5,564	5,564	5,564
12 -Cost Recovery - Personal Property					
13 -					
14 -					
15 =Real Estate Taxable Income	(1,411)	(429)	855	2,213	3,653
16 Tax Liability @ 36% (Savings)	(508)	(154)	308	797	1,315

EXHIBIT NO. 12

Line 13 - 14

These lines are here to accommodate any special items that the investor may wish to include in order to meet his personal investment objectives. They are also provided to accommodate things such as those found on lines 32 - 34 of the APOD, which are Funded Reserves for, say, future carpet or appliances replacement. You might use them to enter Leasing

Commissions payable or any Capital Additions to be subtracted from the NOI.

LINE 15

The figure entered here is the total of all the arithmetic called for in lines 1 - 14. Notice the little add (+), minus (-) and equal (=) signs next to each item. Line 15 then is the total Real Estate Taxable income for that year.

Please notice that our sample property Real Estate Taxable income is minus $1,411 or (-1,411). This means that ALL the income for that year, after deducting the interest payments and the depreciation, is exempt from income taxes with $1,400 of tax shelter left over that can be applied to other investment income.

LINE 16

Assuming that the buyer is in the 36% tax bracket, he then takes the $1411 and applies it to other taxable investment income. He finds that he saved $508 that normally would have gone to Uncle Sam. It is $508 that he would not enjoy, had he not owned this property. Therefore, this $508 of 'extra' income is attributed to the ownership of this property. This is the second of the Tributaries of the Income Stream, the *TAX SHELTER YIELD*.

The Cash Flow Section

The search assignment for the next group of figures, lines 17 - 24, is for the Cash Flow After Taxes. What we're looking for here is, how much real cash did we earn that year after income taxes? Using our sample property and bringing down the information from the above figures we now see that our Cash Flow After Taxes is $3635. This number actually represents a combination of the first two elements of the Income Stream - the *Cash Yield* and the *Tax Shelter Yield*. Filled out for the first years operation our Cash Flow Worksheet will look like this:

17	NET OPERATING INCOME (Line 8)	22,075
18	-Annual Debt Service	18,948
19	-	
20	-	
21	=CASH FLOW BEFORE TAXES	3,127
22	-Tax Liability (Savings) (Line 16)	(508)
23	+Investment Tax Credit	
24	=CASH FLOW AFTER TAXES	$3,635

EXHIBIT NO. 13

Before going on to project what our future income might be in the future YEARS columns on the CFA worksheet, we need to spend a few minutes on what we call the Growth Factor.

THE GROWTH FACTOR

The Growth Factor is an arbitrary number selected by the investor and his real estate counselor or broker and is based on past performance of this and/or similar properties, and on future growth patterns. That is, a factor based on what future rents might reasonably be raised to, or what future vacancy and expense levels may be at that time. Also keep in mind that as rents are raised, so is the value of the property raised commensurably. Obviously, deductions need to made for deterioration, deferred maintenance and functional obsolescence, if any. All of this is congruous with the principle that the income stream establishes value.

Going back to our example, let's suppose the investor anticipated that the rents could be raised at the rate of 5% each year over the next five years, and the expense rate would remain the same percentage level 41% of Gross Operating

Income. (This is hardly ever true for expenses but let's do it this way for now in order to keep our example simple) The Income Growth factor for our example then is 5% per year. The numbers will look like this:

Cash Flow Analysis Worksheet

				Purchase Price	$180,000
Property Name	SAMPLE PROPERTY APTS.			Acquisition Costs	- 0 - (PAID BY SELLER)
Prepared For	SPECIFIC BUYER			Loan Points	- 0 -
Prepared By	M. VESTOR			Down Payment	40,000
Date Prepared	31 DEC 08				

Mortgage Data				Cost Recovery Data		
	1st Mortgage	2nd Mortgage			Improvements	Personal Property
Amount	140,000			Value	153,000	
Interest Rate	13%			C. R. Method	SL	
Term	25			Useful Life	27.5	
Payments/Year	12	12		In Service Date	31 DEC	
Periodic Payment	1,579	-		Recapture		
Annual Debt Service	18,948	-		(All/None/Excess)		
Comments				Investment Tax Credit ($$ or %)		

Taxable Income

	Year :	1	2	3	4	5
1	Potential Rental Income	39,120	41,076	43,130	45,286	47,551
2	+Other Income affected by vacancy					
3	-Vacancy & Credit Losses	1,956	2,054	2,156	2,264	2,378
4	=Effective Rental Income	37,164	39,022	40,973	43,022	45,173
5	+Other Income not affected by vacancy					
6	=Gross Operating Income	37,164	39,022	40,973	43,022	45,173
7	-Operating Expenses	15,089	15,843	16,636	17,467	18,341
8	=NET OPERATING INCOME	22,075	23,179	24,338	25,555	26,832
9	-Interest - 1st Mortgage	18,154	18,044	17,920	17,778	17,616
10	-Interest - 2nd Mortgage					
11	-Cost Recovery - Improvements	5,332	5,564	5,564	5,564	5,564
12	-Cost Recovery - Personal Property					
13	-					
14	-					
15	=Real Estate Taxable Income	(1,411)	(429)	855	2,213	3,653
16	Tax Liability @ 36% (Savings)	(508)	(154)	308	797	1,315

Cash Flows

17	NET OPERATING INCOME (Line 8)	22,075	23,179	24,338	25,555	26,832
18	-Annual Debt Service	18,948	18,948	18,948	18,948	18,948
19	-					
20	-					
21	=CASH FLOW BEFORE TAXES	3,127	4,231	5,390	6,607	7,885
22	-Tax Liability (Savings) (Line 16)	(508)	(154)	308	797	1,315
23	+Investment Tax Credit					
24	=CASH FLOW AFTER TAXES	$3,635	$4,386	$5,082	$5,810	$6,570

The statements and figures herein, while not guaranteed, are secured from sources we believe authoritative.

EXHIBIT NO. 14

SUMMARY OF THE CFA WORKSHEET

Well, to this point we have located the first element of the Income Stream, the CASH YIELD, on the APOD (line 35) and the second element, the TAX SHELTER YIELD, on the CFA (lines 16 and 22), and a combination of both yields (line 24) of the CFA.

The importance of these two information documents and how they work together should now become abundantly clear to the reader. Anything less than this would not be adequate in your search for the total Income Stream.

In projecting and spreading out our numbers for 5 years we are ready to go further in our search for the other two Income Stream Yields:

3- EQUITY INCREASE INCOME
4- APPRECIATION INCOME

To do so we now turn to the ALTERNATIVE CASH SALES WORKSHEET.

CHAPTER 5
IDENTIFYING THE INCOME STREAM ON THE ACS

The third form which we use to analyze real estate investments is the Alternative Cash Sales Worksheet or the ACS.

The assignment for this form is to establish a projected sales price, estimate the tax consequences and show the Capital Gains. On this form we will also find the Equity Build-up and Appreciation yields of the Income Stream.

The two main sections are:

1- MORTGAGE BALANCES

2- CALCULATIONS OF SALES PROCEEDS

Take a moment now and look at a blank ACS on the next page....

Alternative Cash Sales Worksheet

	Mortgage Balances			
Year:				
Principal Balance - 1st Mortgage				
Principal Balance - 2nd Mortgage				
TOTAL UNPAID BALANCE				

Calculation of Sale Proceeds

PROJECTED SALES PRICE

CALCULATION OF ADJUSTED BASIS:
1. Basis at Acquisition
2. + Capital Additions
3. - Cost Recovery (Depreciation) Taken
4. - Basis in Partial Sales
5. =Adjusted Basis at Sale

CALCULATION OF EXCESS COST RECOVERY
6. Total Cost Recovery Taken (Line 3)
7. - Straight Line Cost Recovery
8. =Excess Cost Recovery

CALCULATION OF CAPITAL GAIN ON SALE:
9. Sale Price
10. - Costs of Sale
11. - Adjusted Basis at Sale (Line 5)
12. - Participation Payments
13. =Total Gain
14. - Excess Cost Recovery (Line 8)
15. - Suspended Losses
16. =Gain or (Loss)
17. - Straight Line Cost Recovery (limited to gain)
18. =Capital Gain from Appreciation

ITEMS TAXED AS ORDINARY INCOME:
19. Excess Cost Recovery (Line 8)
20. - Unamortized Loan Points
21. =Ordinary Taxable Income

CALCULATION OF SALE PROCEEDS AFTER TAXES:
22. Sale Price
23. - Cost of Sale
24. - Participation Payments
25. - Mortgage Balance(s)
26. =Sale Proceeds Before Tax
27. - Tax (Savings) Ordinary Income at ____% (Line21)
28. - Tax on Straight Line Recapture at ____% (Line 17)
29. - Tax on Capital Gains at ____% (Line 18)
30. =Sales Proceeds After Taxes

EXHIBIT NO. 15

Looks pretty scarey doesn't it? All those blanks and boxes and questions to be answered. Well, be of good cheer. It's not really that bad. You made it through the APOD and CFA forms didn't you? This one will be a piece of cake also, if we dismantle it and take it one step at the time.

By now you may be asking: Why should I learn about the forms when the computer can do this instantly? The answer is: You need to know the inner workings -- just how these conclusions are arrived at -- in order to give you confidence in the system and to develop your real estate investment skills. Once learned, you will have an extra tool in your investment tool-box that will give you a great advantage over others less skilled.

THE MORTGAGE BALANCES SECTION

This section provides the mortgage balances for our projected investment period. You will also notice in our filled out form (page 67) an extra line entitled: Equity Build-up EOY (end of year). This is to show the amount of equity gained by paying down the mortgage for that year.

These figures represent yield number three of the four yields of the income stream -- The Equity Build-up yield, but before taxes. Taxes will be considered when this yield is combined with the Appreciation yield coming up.

THE CALCULATIONS OF SALES PROCEEDS SECTION

This section begins with a request for a Projected Sales Price. Where do we get that number? How do we arrive at a sales price that is five years off?

The system in use today is to pick a reasonable market capitalization rate (usually selected from sales of similar properties) and capitalize the sixth year NOI as projected on our CFA worksheet.

The reason we see several columns on the ACS form is so that we may try several cap rates to help us arrive at a reasonably projected sales price.

Placing that system aside for a moment, let's take a look at another technique that we recommend. You will recall that

The Value of a Property is Determined by the Value of the Income Stream. Based on this premise it is reasonable to assume that, as the income grows, so grows the overall value of the property.

We projected an income growth factor of 5% a year for our sample property. Based on that, a 5% a year increase in value should occur; so we simply compound our beginning price by that number to give us a starting price. We realize that we must still meet the market cap rate test in order to be somewhere in line with the market.

Sample Property Computations:

Year 1 $180,000 + 5% = 189,000

2 $189,000 + 5% = 198,450

3 $198,450 + 5% = 208,372

4 $208,372 + 5% = 218,791

5 $218,791 + 5% = 229,730

Fifth Year Value Est. Say $230,000

Now to make the cap rate test we need to go to the sample property CFA (page 56) and bring forth the sixth year

NOI. Oh yeah, right, we don't have a sixth year NOI because our projection only went for 5 years. Well, what we do is simply take the fifth year NOI and increase it by our growth factor of 5%.

Year 5 NOI $26,832 + 5% = 28,173

Sixth year NOI $28,173

To complete the cap rate search we then multiply the sixth year NOI by the estimated value above:

$28,173 Divided by 230,000 = 12.25%

In our example, upon examining the market, we find that 12% seems to be an acceptable cap rate. We multiply our 6th year NOI by 12% and reach a sales price of $234,787 to use in our Sample Property ACS.

Let's return now to the currently used method of trying to find a suggested sales price by use of the sixth year NOI ($28,173) and an experimental cap rate. Let's try 13, 11 & 10 and see what we come up with.

Projected Sales Price $\underline{\$216,715}$ $\underline{\$256,127}$ $\underline{\$281,739}$

Cap Rate Used   13%   11%   10%

Did you notice that the higher the cap rate the lower the price and the lower the cap rate the higher the price? Of course as a seller you want it as low as you can get it and as a buyer you want it as high as you can get it. That's why we have to be reasonable in trying to find out what the market will bear. We seem to be pretty close at 12% as it appears to coincide with our growth factor.

LOOKING AT THE ACS FORM LINE BY LINE

Calculations of Adjusted Basis (Lines 1-5)

The information to be determined here is to show what your Tax Basis is for this property, that is, how much Cost Recovery (depreciation) you have used and how much you have left. Keep in mind that your Basis at Acquisition is always the purchase price.

Calculation of Excess Cost Recovery (Lines 6-8)

The purpose here is to determine if you have taken more Cost Recovery than is allowable. Only Straight Line Cost Recovery is permissible.

Calculation of Capital Gain on Sale (Lines 9-18)

The primary search assignment for this section is to determine the amount of Capital Gain earned at this projected sale price. It is also to separate the Capital Gain from that which is earned through Cost Recovery and that earned by appreciation of value.

The reason for the separation is that while the Federal Government may have recently lowered the Capital Gains rate to 20% it also placed a tax on the used up Straight Line Cost Recovery. The Straight Line Cost Recovery tax rate is 25%. We will see these computations as we advance further in the ACS form.

Items Taxed As Ordinary Income (Lines 19-21)

Had you used more Cost Recovery than allowed (line 8 above) this is where you compute the tax owed. Excess Cost

Recovery is taxed at the ordinary income rate . Notice that this is where you may deduct any unamortized loan points.

Calculation Of Sales Proceeds After Tax (Lines 22-30)

This section is where the real action is. It brings together all the computations made above, shows the tax consequences of the sale and gives us the Sales Proceeds After Taxes.

Please take notice of the little add (+) or minus (-) signs immediately to the right of the item number. This is to help you know what is taking place.

The Sales Proceeds After Taxes is a combination of yields 3 and 4 of the Income Stream.

To demonstrate the ACS form we have filled one in using our sample property. See the next page.

Alternative Cash Sales Worksheet

SAMPLE PROPERTY
10 UNIT APT.

Mortgage Balances

	Year:	1	2	3	4	5
Principal Balance - 1st Mortgage		139,206	138,303	137,275	136,105	134,773
Principal Balance - 2nd Mortgage						
TOTAL UNPAID BALANCE		139,206	138,303	137,275	136,105	134,773
EQUITY BUILD-UP E.O.Y.		749	903	1,028	1,170	1,332

Calculation of Sale Proceeds

PROJECTED SALES PRICE	234,783	256,127	281,739
6TH YR NOI 28,174	12% CAP RATE	11% CAP RATE	10% CAP RATE

CALCULATION OF ADJUSTED BASIS:				
1	Basis at Acquisition	$ 180,000	$180,000	$180,000
2	+ Capital Additions			
3	- Cost Recovery (Depreciation) Taken	27,586	27,586	27,586
4	- Basis in Partial Sales			
5	=Adjusted Basis at Sale	152,414	152,414	152,414
CALCULATION OF EXCESS COST RECOVERY				
6	Total Cost Recovery Taken (Line 3)	27,586	27,586	27,586
7	- Straight Line Cost Recovery	27,586	27,586	27,586
8	=Excess Cost Recovery	0	0	0
CALCULATION OF CAPITAL GAIN ON SALE:				
9	Sale Price	234,783	256,127	281,739
10	- Costs of Sale	16,435	17,929	19,722
11	- Adjusted Basis at Sale (Line 5)	152,414	152,414	152,414
12	- Participation Payments			
13	=Total Gain	65,934	85,784	109,604
14	- Excess Cost Recovery (Line 8)	0	0	0
15	- Suspended Losses			
16	=Gain or (Loss)	65,934	85,784	109,604
17	- Straight Line Cost Recovery (limited to gain)	27,586	27,586	27,586
18	=Capital Gain from Appreciation	38,348	58,148	82,018
ITEMS TAXED AS ORDINARY INCOME:				
19	Excess Cost Recovery (Line 8)	0	0	0
20	- Unamortized Loan Points			
21	=Ordinary Taxable Income	0	0	0
CALCULATION OF SALE PROCEEDS AFTER TAXES:				
22	Sale Price (line 9)	234,783	256,127	281,739
23	- Cost of Sale (line 10)	16,435	17,929	19,722
24	- Participation Payments (line 12)			
25	- Mortgage Balance(s)	134,773	134,773	134,773
26	=Sale Proceeds Before Tax	83,575	103,425	127,244
27	- Tax (Savings) Ordinary Income at ___ % (Line 21)			
28	- Tax on Straight Line Recapture at 25 % (Line 17)	6,897	6,897	6,897
29	- Tax on Capital Gains at 20 % (Line 18)	7,670	11,640	16,404
30	=Sales Proceeds After Taxes	$ 69,009	$ 84,888	$103,943

EXHIBIT NO. 16

SUMMARY OF THE ACS WORKSHEET

We have now successfully located all four yield elements (tributaries) of the Income Stream on the property information documents.

1-CASH YIELD

> on the APOD Worksheet-line 35
>
> on the CFA Worksheet-line 21

2-TAX SHELTER YIELD

> on the CFA Worksheet-lines 16 & 22

3-EQUITY BUILD-UP YIELD

> on the ACS Worksheet- 4th line from the top

4-APPRECIATION YIELD

> on the ACS Worksheet- line 26 after subtracting the original cash down payment and the equity build-up for the investment period.

Our next effort will be to combine all the yield elements into one single rate of return and then with that rate of return establish a value of the property.

CHAPTER 6

INTRODUCTION TO THE INTERNAL RATE OF RETURN IRR
UNDERSTANDING RULES OF THUMB

Up to this point we have identified the four elements (or tributaries) of the Income Stream and how to find them on the offering documents.

We will now describe the process of valuation of the Income Stream. This is the most interesting and revealing bit of information we have to offer. Exciting in content and revolutionary in form, it invalidates all previous methods of investment real estate analysis.

RULES OF THUMB

Over the years investors have used a variety of methods to determine the value of real estate. But only in the last ten or fifteen years have we adopted the discounted cash flow and the Internal Rate of Return (IRR) system. Though rapidly gaining popularity, it is still not universally used by most real estate practitioners. It is not easy to understand and takes some effort to accumulate information needed to make calculations and then work throught a myriad of variations. But when it is complete, the mystery of real estate investment is reduced to the specific levels of performance that must be acheived in order to obtain a desired return, taking all tributaries of the income stream into consideration. With the help of good calculators and ever-evolving computer software the ability of the average investor to produce this very valuable information is greatly enhanced.

This IRR system superceeds all other systems thus far contrived. This includes such popular rules of thumb as: "Cash on Cash", the "Broker's Rate", the "Gross Rent Multiplier", the "Square Foot Index", and the "Capitalization Rate".

WEAKNESSES OF "THUMB-RULES"

THEY DO NOT:

.... consider the impact of financing.

.... provide for future income variation.

.... consider income tax consequences.

.... apply to properties with negative income.

.... consider potential appreciation.

It's clear that an investor would be foolish to buy a property based on "rules of thumb". They don't give enough information. A property with great first year income may look good on the surface, but could lead to financial suicide. Conversely, a property producing zero or negative income the first few years could prove a bonanza in later years.

Your best bet is to steer clear of thumb rules when making final investment decision. Instead, assemble and analyze the property information. This could make the difference between success and failure.

OLD HABITS DIE HARD

Did it ever occur to you why there are so many different "rules of thumb" for investment real estate? It's because they are imprecise. I used to use the old systems religiously, but with an uneasy feeling deep down inside that they lacked something. That something is the discounted cash flow / internal rate of return system (IRR). This new method feels correct and complete. It has never failed me.

THE ROLE OF THE "THUMB RULES" TODAY

Before we "throw the baby out with the bath water," let us explain that the "rules of thumb" still play a minor role in real estate investment analysis, we use them for several purposes. Some of these are:

> 1- As a quick method to determine whether or not an investment is worthy of further analysis.

2- As a tool to determine demographics.

3- To develop market studies of comparable properties.

4- As an appraisal tool to arrive at a real estate property value.

Let's examine some of the "thumb rules" and explain how they work.

THE 'PRICE PER' INDEX

The "Price Per" Index includes:
- Price per room
- Price per square foot
- Price per unit
- Price per acre

These usually apply to the following investment types:

Multi-Family (Apartments)	- Price per unit
Hotel/Motel	- Price per room
Office Space	- Price per square foot
Retail Space	- Price per square foot
Industrial Space	- Price per square foot
Land	- Price per acre

The "Price Per" Index is arrived at by dividing the unit used (i.e. square foot, number of rooms, etc ...) into the asking price for the investment.

Examples

- A 175 unit apartment house is being offered for $3,500,000. The price per unit is $20,000.

- A 100 room motel is offered at $2,790,000. The price per room is $27,900.

- An 8,900 square foot strip shopping center is being offered for $607,500. The price per square foot is $68.26.

THE 'CASH -ON- CASH' METHOD

Another popular rule of thumb is the 'Cash - On - Cash' method. This system relates the Cash PAID IN to the Cash Income COMING OUT of the property. By dividing the income by the purchase price you may establish the yield rate and thus the value of the property.

Now you can see the weakness and shortsightedness of

the above systems, though there are some people who still use them. Many investors are aware of the other yields of the Income Stream but do not yet trust them. They figure that if the CASH ON CASH yield is adequate then the rest of the yields will just be 'gravy'.

Here is the problem with that thinking: a knowledgeable seller -- who is aware of the value of all four elements of the Income Stream -- will price his property to reflect ALL of its values.

INTRODUCING IRV

We need to talk about IRV in order to understand "CAPITALIZING", that is, placing a value on an income stream.

In IRV I = Income, R = Rate of Return, and V = the Value of the item being capitalized. IRV is a simple technique to help us find an unknown element of IRV when the other two are known. If you know two of the elements of IRV, then the third one can easily be found. Using the IRV Formula to find an income, we set it up like this:

$$I = RV \quad \text{or} \quad \underline{Income} = \text{Rate of Return } X \text{ Value}$$
$$\$700 = 7\% \ X \ 10{,}000$$

Or to find a <u>yield Rate</u> use the formula $R = Income / Value$
$$7\% = 700 \div 10{,}000$$

Or to find a <u>Value</u> use a formula
Value = Income $\div$ Rate of Return
$$10{,}000 = 700 \div 7\%$$

As we shall see, the R in IRV not only stands for the rate of return, but it is also the CAPITALIZATION RATE.

THE CAPITALIZATION RATE (CAP RATE)

The CAP RATE can be used in any situation where you have an income stream and an asking price. The CAP RATE of a real estate investment property is arrived at by dividing the Net Operating Income (NOI, line 30 of the APOD) by the asking price (as we have just seen in IRV). Keep in mind that the Net Operating Income (NOI) is always calculated AFTER vacancies, credit losses, and operating expenses. It is also the income figure BEFORE the mortgage payments, personal taxes and cost recovery.

Examples

- The Net Operating Income of an apartment complex is $39,500. The asking price is $355,500, By dividing the asking price by the Net Operating Income (NOI) we find the cap rate, 9%.

- The NOI of a motel is $125,000, the asking price is $975,000. Dividing the asking price by the Net Operating Income (NOI), the cap rate is 7.8%

We will see more of the Cap Rate later when we discuss appraisal techniques.

These calculations demonstrate that "thumb rules" may help a prospective buyer determine whether to look further into the property. But they should never be used as the sole determinant in deciding whether or not to invest.

INTRODUCTION TO THE INTERNAL RATE OF RETURN (IRR)

Now, techniques for evaluating investment real estate

have become comparable to those used to determine the value of nearly all other investment forms. This superior process is a product of years of research by some of the best professional real estate minds in America. It constitutes a major breakthrough in the field of real estate investing and is just beginning to come into its own as the most valid of all investment tools now generally available. Called the DISCOUNTED CASH FLOW (DCF) Analysis System, it embraces the Internal Rate of Return (IRR) Analysis and the Net Present Value (NPV) Analysis.

While these systems are not learned instantly, they are easily within the reach of anyone who wants to know. Once understood, it can instantly become the standard by which all investments are judged. It will be the most useful tool for those who would take the time to learn. This system is currently being used by the Commercial Investment Real Estate Institute of the National Association of Realtors (NAR) and by many investment brokers and business planners.

In our "whirlwind" society we like quick and easy answers to complex problems. Unfortunately, in the field of investment real estate there are no valid quick and easy ways to determine the worthiness of an investment. The purpose of this book, however, is to simplify this process as much as possible so that almost anyone can gain an understanding. Our effort is to explain each point in sufficient detail to give you enough information to understand what you are reading in a property offering document. Obviously, as you become more familiar with the system it becomes easier to use, and the more fascinating the world of investing.

DISCOUNTED CASH FLOW - WHAT IS IT?

Discounted Cash Flow (DCF) is simply a method of computing returns on investments which is similar to that used in computing interest rates on borrowings. In reality DCF is simply the reciprocal of compound interest. Effectively, it is the reverse of compound interest. It is used in exercising the concept of the 'Time Value' of money

THE CONCEPT OF 'TIME VALUE' OF MONEY

This concept is established on the philosophy that money must be earning at all times and while it is out it should not only be earning but also adequately compensating for several other things. Here are some:

1 - The earnings foregone by giving up the opportunity to invest elsewhere so as to earn interest for one year.

2 - The risk that you may not receive the money one year from today or ever.

3 - Change in the purchasing power of the dollar between today and a year from today.

These and other considerations need to be factored into your anticipated interest rate.

The DCF is probably best explained by this example.

Suppose you are offered the opportunity to buy the right to receive $1,100 one year from now. You want to see that your risk is covered and receive a good return on your money while it is gone. You decide, therefore, that you must earn 10%

interest. What would you pay for that right? $1,000 of course, so when the $1,100 is returned to you, it would include the $1,000 you paid plus the 10% interest, or $100. What has happened is that you <u>discounted</u> the future CASH FLOW by the amount of interest that you required. It is that simple.

NET PRESENT VALUE - WHAT IS IT?

Net Present Value really means what it says. What is the *present value* of a future payment? Using the example above, it is the $1,000 you pay today for the right to receive $1,100, one year from now on the premise that you would earn 10% for that period. The Net Present Value is thus $1,000.

Had you desired an 8% return on your money, the Net Present Value of the income would be $1,018.52, or if you wanted a yield of 12%, the Net Present Value would be $982.14. The process is simply to discount the future yield by the interest desired.

THE BEGINNING OF UNDERSTANDING

We have now reached "the beginning of understanding" of this valuable system of Real Estate Investment Analysis when we:

1- Learn that the income stream is the heart of the investment,

2- Identify the "four yields" of investment real estate,

3- Learn to read and fill out the APOD, the CFA, the ACS worksheets,

4- Locate the "four yields" on the offering documents,

5- Talk about "thumb rules"

6- Understand Discounted Cash Flow (DCF) and Net Present Value (NPV)

Our next and final step is to reduce the total of all the yields of the Income Stream to a single figure which will establish the overall value of the Income Stream of an investment.

CHAPTER 7

THE INTERNAL RATE OF RETURN

We will now introduce you to the "Internal Rate of Return" analysis system. We begin with the "Tee Bar."

THE "TEE BAR"

The "Tee Bar" is two simple lines drawn to form a T upon which we hang out, in effect, all our "in-puts" and "in-comes" from our investment for easy viewing. Using the yields from our 10-unit apartment example, we place them on the "Tee Bar." They should look like this:

Periods	Yields	
0	(40,000)	Original Investment
1	3,635	
2	4,386	
3	5,082	
4	5,810	
5	6,570 + 69,009	Sale Proceeds

The numbers on the left side of the Tee Bar (O through 5) and listed under "periods" correspond with the number of years on the CFA worksheet from which the projection is made. The numbers on the right side, listed under "yields," are the annual Cash Flow After Taxes yield figures taken from line 24 of the CFA worksheet. At the top of the YIELD column, or ground "O", or beginning place, we put the amount of the original investment. In our example it is $40,000. You will notice that we place brackets ( ) around this amount to show that it is an "in-put" figure, as opposed to those without brackets, which show they are "in-come" or yield figures.

At the end of the 5th year, you will notice we have placed the "Sale Proceeds" after tax income figure of $69,009 (see line 30 of the ACS worksheet, page 67) next to the final year's income figure. This is to show what the total income would be if the investment were sold at that time, assuming that the sale occurred on December 31 of the fifth year.

HOW TO SHOW A "NEGATIVE" YIELD

If the investment loses money any one year and the owner must make a contribution, then it will be shown as a negative yield and will have brackets placed around it.

EXAMPLE:

Suppose in the third year you had a bad year with many vacancies due to the nearby industrial plant closing. To meet expenses you had to "in-put" an additional $800 that year. The "Tee Bar" would be set-up like this:

Periods	Yields	
0	(40,000)	Original Investment
1	3,635	
2	4,385	
3	(800)	
4	5,810	
5	6,570	+ 69,009 Sale Proceeds

The Tee Bar, in effect, graphically displays "what goes in" and "what comes out" of the investment. The Tee Bar is a very important part of our understanding the investment yields. It should always be used when exploring any investment. Later on we will learn more of its value, particularly as it applies to other investment types.

HOW TO BRING THE COMBINED YIELDS DOWN TO ONE SINGLE RATE OF RETURN

This is the step we have been waiting for. This is the net result of all the work thus far expended. This is the reason we have an APOD worksheet, a CFA worksheet, an ACS worksheet, the Tee Bar and all the other devices discussed so far. All of these are to help us organize our understanding so that we may arrive at a single value figure.

As previously mentioned, it is not our intent to go deeply into the very involved theory behind these techniques, but rather to show you HOW it works. This will allow you to get quickly into its use.

A deeper understanding can come later if you so desire. This is the shortest 'shortcut' you can make if you plan on exposing your hard-earned dollars to a real estate investment, or, as we shall see, to any other investment type.

To lay the foundation for further understanding, we offer a few examples that will, at first, seem unrelated, but bear with us.

THE INSTALLMENT LOAN PATTERN

In every "lending/repayment in installments with interest" situation there is a certain pattern. It is called the "Installment Loan Pattern." The pattern is that there are always four elements involved. They are:

1. Loan amount.
2. Number of repayments.
3. Amount of each payment.
4. Interest rate.

A very significant rule to remember because it applies directly to our situation is, "If three of these elements are known, the fourth one can be found."

EXAMPLE

You go to the bank and borrow $2,000. You promise to pay back the loan in twelve months. The annual interest rate is 12%. The banker knowing (1) the loan amount, (2) the number of repayments, and (4) the interest rate, will then pull out his little financial calculator and show you that your payments (3) are $177.70. On the Tee Bar, it looks like this to the banker, who considers this loan an investment for his bank:

Periods	Yields	
0	(2,000)	
1	177.70	
2	177.70	
3	177.70	
4	177.70	
5	177.70	
6	177.70	12% Interest rate annually
7	177.70	
8	177.70	
9	177.70	
10	177.70	
11	177.70	
12	177.70	

If you look closely you can see the four elements of the "Installment Loan Pattern" within the example. The $2000 is #1, Loan Amount. The periods from 1 to 12 comprise #2, the number of repayments. The $177.70 is #3, Amount of Payments. The 12% figure is #4, Interest rate.

Had you told the banker that you wanted to borrow $2000 and you could pay $177.70 for 12 months he could go to his little calculator again and show you that the interest rate would be 12%.

Had you told him you would be willing to pay 12% annual interest and could make payments of $177.70 for 12 Months he would, again, tell you instantly that the total amount to be borrowed would be $2000. If three of the elements are known the fourth one can be found.

MATCHING UP THE INSTALLMENT LOAN PATTERN WITH THE INVESTMENT PATTERN

It is interesting to note here that an investment and its resultant yields, as laid out on the "Tee Bar," will follow a pattern which will almost exactly match the "Installment Loan Pattern."

We call this arrangement of investment criteria "The Investment Pattern". After all, is an investor not, in effect, tying up his money in anticipation of a periodical return with interest? Isn't that really what an investment is?

THE ELEMENTS MATCH UP LIKE THIS:

THE INSTALLMENT LOAN PATTERN	THE INVESTMENT PATTERN
1. Loan Amount	1. Original Investment
2. Number of repayments	2. Number of years of ownership
3. Amount of each payments	3. Annual yields + Sales proceeds
4. Interest rate	4. Yield rate (rate of return)

When viewed this way the whole process becomes a very significant tool in valuating investment yield rates from real estate or from any other investment type for that matter. Let's take a look at some examples:

Example 1- A Mortgage

You sell your house and take back a second mortgage as part of your equity. What you are really doing is effectively lending the buyer money to buy your house. Therefore, this is set up as an Installment Loan. The principal amount is $2950. You want market interest of 10%. The buyer can only afford to pay $100 per month. Your Realtor enters the figure, into his financial calculator and finds that the time period is 34 months. On the 'tee' bar it looks like this:

Periods	Yields	
0	(2,950)	
1	100	
2	100	
3	100	**10% Annual Rate** Of Return
|	100	
33	100	
34	100	

By knowing three of the elements of the INSTALLMENT LOAN PATTERN the fourth can be found easily.

The same thing is pretty close to what happens with the INVESTMENT PATTERN when searching for a yield rate, with a couple of minor exceptions. Here is the difference. By knowing 3 of the elements of the investment pattern you can find the 4th. However, 2 of the known factors must be the number of periods and their yields. The reason is that in the investment pattern the annual yields are usually for <u>different</u> <u>amounts</u>. And the overall yield rate, while a true annual yield rate for the length of the investment, is not the yield rate for each year, but rather the average per year over the life of the investment. Let's take another example using different payment rates.

Periods	Yields	
0	($5,000)	Original Investment
1	1100	
2	800	___Rate of Return
3	2000	
4	2100	
5	1200	+ 1850 Sales Proceeds

We now know three of the elements: 1- the original investment, 2- the number years of ownership, and 3- the annual yields plus sales proceeds. Knowing three elements (one of which is not the yield rate), we now can find the fourth -- the annual rate of return. How do we do this? The same principles apply.

As explained, the only difference is that the payments are not all equal. It therefore requires a little more computation, a more involved financial calculator. What is really happening here is that the calculator will consider the cash flow as it is discounted because it is received at a later time. The calculator will then annualize the yields into one averaged figure even though that will not necessarily be the yield for any one year. Because of this the annual yield rate is no longer called the Interest Rate but rather the Internal Rate of Return (IRR).

At the end of this chapter we will give you details concerning the special type of financial calculator required to make these computations and a further definition of the IRR. Again, you consult your calculator or your realtor, or anyone else who has the calculator with this capacity. After you enter the three known elements, it will shortly give you the fourth. Using the above example we see that the averaged annual rate of return or IRR for our example is 19%.

EXAMPLE #2 - 10 UNIT APARTMENT

Now let's go back to the sample property we used in filling out the APOD, the CFA, the ACS worksheets and the original "Tee Bar" (page 84) to determine just what our yield is on this example.

Periods	Yields	
0	(40,000)	Original Investment
1	3,635	
2	4,386	**21.5% IRR**
3	5,082	
4	5,810	
5	6,570	+ 69,009 Sales Proceeds

Again we resort to the slightly more sophisticated calculator because we have irregular amounts in the PAYMENTS (or yields) portion of our problem. After entering our figures we instantly learn that the yield from our investment is 21.5% per year averaged over the projected life of the investment. Because this yield, while averaged over the life of the investment, is not, in fact, the yield for any one particular year, it is called the Internal Rate of Return, the IRR for short.

You might well ask by this time, "What was the discount rate used to discount those future cash flows?" That's a good question. The answer is found in the definition of just what an Internal Rate of Return is. Let's try it. Here are three definitions that the author has collected over the years, the source of which is long since forgotten. They say pretty much the same thing only in different ways, but they are all correct.

THE IRR DEFINED

The IRR is:

"THE YIELD RATE THAT EQUATES THE PRESENT VALUE OF ALL CASH FLOWS WITH THE INITIAL CASH EQUITY."

or

THE IRR MAY BE DEFINED AS "THAT RATE OF DISCOUNT AT WHICH THE PRESENT WORTH OF FUTURE CASH FLOWS IS EXACTLY EQUAL TO THE INITIAL CAPITAL INVESTMENT."

or

"A METHOD OF ANALYSIS WHICH INDICATES THE RATE OF RETURN WHICH EQUATES THE PRESENT VALUE OF FUTURE BENEFITS TO THE PRESENT VALUE OF THE INVESTMENT OUTLAY. AN ANALYTICAL MEASUREMENT OF PROFITABILITY OF AN INVESTMENT WHICH CONSIDERS NOT ONLY THE AMOUNT OF PROFITS BUT

ALSO THAT POINT OR THOSE POINTS IN TIME WHEN THE PROFIT IS RECEIVED."

This may tend to be a little confusing to some, but, be of good cheer. This is some of that higher learning for those who may wish to go deeper into real estate investment analysis mentioned earlier. The primary objective of this book is to give you a basis for understanding.

Now, getting back to the Investment Pattern compared to the Installment Loan Pattern: The difference between the simple annual interest rate figure and the Internal Rate of Return (IRR) figure is that the IRR figure is an after-tax amount and reflects the overall income (or yield) earned averaged over the life of the investment. The actual income (or yield) earned for any particular year may, or may not coincide precisely with the IRR. However, it does not diminish the fact that the IRR, as the overall yield, is indeed a correct after-tax yield rate and contains all four yield elements of the Income Stream.

It is important to note here that both yield rates, the IRR and the interest rate, are all-inclusive in that they both include the return <u>OF</u> the original capital and the return <u>ON</u> the original capital. This is something seriously lacking in any other system, particularly those previously used to valuate investment real estate, especially in the so-called "rules of thumb," previously used for valuing properties erroneously for so many years.

Effectively, what we have done is reduce the entire Income Stream, including all of its tributaries into one single value, the IRR. The question now is, How do we arrive at an "Overall" value for the property for you personally, putting aside the asking price or the appraised price? To do this we go to the next chapter 'Valuing the Real Estate Using the Income Stream.'

CALCULATORS OF THE IRR

The main manufacturers of the financial calculators required to reach the IRR are the Hewlett-Packard Company and the Texas Instruments Company. Their products are found in most office supply stores. The model numbers are as follows:

Hewlett-Packard -   38E, 12C, 10B, 17BII, 19BII
Texas Instruments   BA-2II Plus
                    BA-Real Estate
                    BA-35 Solar

CHAPTER 8
VALUING THE REAL ESTATE USING
THE INCOME STREAM

Thinking back to the earlier pages of this work you will recall the important investment truism that says THE VALUE OF AN INVESTMENT PROPERTY IS DETERMINED BY ITS INCOME. You probably have noticed also that in the analysis system INCOME is evaluated on various levels such as the Net Operating Income (NOI), the Cash Flow Before Taxes and the Cash Flow After Taxes.

Today, the most common method of income property

evaluation is by using the NOI. Keep in mind that the NOI is the income calculated after expenses but before mortgage payments, depreciation and tax consequences.

HOW TO USE THE NET OPERATING INCOME (NOI) TO ESTIMATE A PROPERTY VALUE

In order to arrive at a value of the real estate using this method we need to look at the projected Net Operating Income (NOI). This is found on the CFA line 8 or 17. In our illustration we will call upon the figures as projected in our sample property for a selected number of years on our CFA.

We will also need to obtain a reliable overall capitalization rate from the market which represents a property with comparable characteristics such as location, size, age and type of tenancy. We will use a cap rate of 17% for this illustration.

The steps to determine property value are:

1- Select a cap rate (discount rate)

2- Discount each year's NOI by the cap rate

3- Discount the resale figure by the cap rate

4- Add them all together

This will give you the total Estimated Value based on the Discounted Cash Flow and resale price.

YEAR	NOI With Growth Rate of 5%	Resale	Present Value at 17%
1	22,075		$18,868
2	23,179		16,933
3	24,338		15,196
4	25,555		13,637
5	26,832		12,238
5		234,783	107,087
		Est Value Total	$183,959

As you can see we have arrived at a price for the property that is pretty close to the $180,000 figure asked for our sample property by using this method.

You will notice also that the discount cap rate (or desired

yield rate) of 17% is not very close to the 21.5% Internal Rate of Return (IRR) arrived at in our example. That is simply because when we use the NOI we have not yet included the benefits of leverage, depreciation or the tax shelter income. In effect, this shows us an estimated value <u>before</u> mortgage and <u>before</u> taxes.

In a strict sense valuing the real estate itself and valuing the Income Stream are two different things. What's the difference? The difference is that when you value the real estate using today's method you use only the NOI as explained above. The NOI simply does not include ALL the income sources of the Income Stream. This is one reason why the so-called appraised value is of limited use to the investor who has his eye on the total Income Stream.

So when you get down to it, the estimate of value, no matter how it was arrived at, will have but little value to you. Here's another reason why;

THE APPRAISAL IS AN ESTIMATE OF VALUE - BUT IN REALITY YOU SET THE PRICE

In appraising property or estimating value, keep in mind that an appraisal is only a Range of Value within which a price may usually be found. Appraisals are not absolutes. Appraising is NOT an exact science.

In the final analysis the real value of a property is what a ready, willing, able and informed buyer is prepared to pay for it at that particular moment in time. In other words, as a buyer, you pay what the property is worth to you. Never mind asking prices, appraisals, what the owner paid for it, or whatever.

Look at the income stream as it affects your tax situation and meets your investment objectives. Analyze the income stream, arrive at your own purchase price and make an offer based on that.

HOW TO ARRIVE AT A VALUE TO SUIT YOUR PERSONAL IRR

First off you will need to be able to determine just how much IRR is adequate for your level of investment comfort. Of course the watchword is always get as much as you can, but realistically the question is how little can you take and still make a reasonable return ON and a return OF the original investment.

At this point not only will the income be a part of the decision but also a lot of other things. Things such as the amount of risk taken, liquidity, growth potential, the competition of similar investments, the tax advantages, personal management time required, etc. Based on these things you must establish your own comfort level and therefore your own IRR. This will become easier as you get into specific properties and begin to understand the variables which will, in fact, constitute the risk.

The way to arrive at a value to suit your investment criteria using the IRR is done simply by filling out the APOD, CFA and ACS forms using the price at which the property is being offered and then fill in your own variables and growth rate. If the IRR is not adequate to meet your requirements then keep adjusting the price until your IRR appears.

HOW DO WE VALUE AN EXISTING PROPERTY USING THE IRR

If you currently own a property and wish to value it using

this method you simply return to the APOD, CFA and ACS worksheets and gather your data.

To begin this you will need to pull a suggested price for the property out of the air (somewhere close to what comparable properties might sell for). With that you can start the analysis process, using reasonable projections where needed, and see what kind of IRR your property can and does produce based on the hypothetical price. If the IRR appears too low to interest a possible buyer then lower the price and do it again. If the IRR appears to be unreasonably high then raise the price and try again.

By manipulating the price and finding a reasonable IRR you can begin to arrive at a good clear market value. You are probably asking about now: What is a 'reasonable' IRR ?. . . .Good question. . . Just keep in mind that the buyer wants it as high as possible and you want it as low as possible. What you do now is NEGOTIATE until you and your buyer are satisfied. At least now, with the IRR in place, you know that ALL the elements of the Income Stream are being considered and are part of the value.

Now let's talk about one of the great bugaboos of real estate, the over-priced property.

THE OVERPRICED PROPERTY

Today, in the world of Commercial / Investment real estate we find that nearly ALL properties available for sale are OVERPRICED. These are therefore hard to sell and contribute greatly to the reason why real estate has a bad reputation for not being liquid.

Before we explain why, let's consider what happens when an overpriced property is placed on the market.

1- Due to it's overpricing, the property remains on the market an extraordinary length of time, losing valuable sales momentum. The owner becomes frustrated and begins his journey from agent to agent, each time lowering the price a little, hoping to find that willing buyer

2- Agents taking the overpriced listing will spend hundreds, maybe thousands, of dollars in advertising and promotion. Plus many, many valuable hours showing the property and wasting the time and confidence otherwise qualified buyers

3- Good prospective buyers will bypass overpriced properties and spend their time on properties that make some sense or at least close to it.

The real problem here is that the owner / seller has no idea of the market value of his property. And, because of this uncertainty, he places a very high price on it in hopes that buyers will come along and make enough offers to help him know what the real market value is. Or he waits until a price comes along that 'feels good' but has no basis in reality.

Remember the real market value is -- "What a ready, willing, able, and informed buyer is willing to pay at that point in time."

The purpose of this discussion is to help point out the absolute necessity of getting your property analyzed before placing it on the market. In doing so you will clarify the income stream of your income property and thereby show its real value, not only to you as the owner but also to a prospective buyer.

When a prospective buyer can clearly see a chance to make a reasonable return on his investment, considering all his risks involved, he will be more apt to go forward. The seller then can be comfortable that he got a good, fair market price.

Any knowledgeable broker will tell you that those properties with a clearly demonstrated income stream and a reasonable chance to continue in like manner will sell very quickly.

At this point some of you may be thinking about those lonely old buildings or parcels of land in almost every town that sit around without tenants and therefore no income. How do we handle them using this system? Well obviously you can't but that doesn't necessarily mean "NO income = NO value." There is value but it cannot be counted on until you can find a use and a tenant.

CHAPTER 9

THE VARIABLES OF THE
INVESTMENT ANALYSIS PROCESS
LIQUIDITY AND RISK

Some of the reasons people do not invest in real estate are centered around these three seemingly negative qualities: lack of liquidity, high risk and involved personal management. It will be helpful if we take some time now to discuss the first two. Management will be covered in chapter 11.

LET'S TALK ABOUT LIQUIDITY

The definition of liquidity in a financial sense is the ability to convert an asset back to cash. Probably a more sensible definition would be the ability to get all the money back that you paid into an investment. This would certainly be the way to look at it if you were an investor who paid $100 for a share of stock and its value was down to $50. His stock then, would not be too liquid unless he wanted to take his loss. As a practical matter he would probably hold the stock with the anticipation that it might go back up again to at least what he paid for it. The question is, Where is the so-called liquidity? It seems pretty safe to conclude that the stock investment is liquid only if it is going up or remaining stagnant.

Without question, real estate is not as liquid as stocks and bonds; however, it is not as illiquid as some would have you believe. Like the stock, it will sell at some price if the owner is willing to take less than what he paid for it if the value is not rising.

The need to liquidate something instantly is a bit of foolishness promulgated by many of those who sell securities. "Invest with us," they say, "and you have instant liquidity." How often in a lifetime of the vast majority of us have we ever had to liquidate instantly, to have all of our assets converted to cash? Almost never. This is like saying that a person of financial means has no power to raise money. This is simply not true unless he has dramatically over extended himself or has poor credit. This doesn't really characterize a wise investor who follows the rules of diversified portfolio which include having cash on hand for emergencies. Of course the exceptions are those rare tragedies which we hope none of us will have. The solution again is to stay adequately insured.

LET'S TALK ABOUT RISK

To a great extent Risk, as it is so called, is the reason many people do not use real estate as an investment medium. Unfortunately, purveyors of other investment types have, in effect, branded real estate as a high risk investment and placed unwarranted fear in the hearts of many who could otherwise enjoy the benefits of this, the most profitable of all investments. True, in its purest sense, there is risk in all investments. It is also true that nearly every investment type or form has within it some offerings that contain greater risk than others. This is also very true in real estate. To classify all forms of investment real estate as "Risky" is extremely shortsighted. For every stock, bond or retirement plan offered there can be a comparable real estate investment that could yield better and yet be safer than the safest corporate stock or bond offered. Here is an example.

Example:

Suppose Aunt Minnie died and left you with $100,000. You enter the investment market and spend $50,000 on General Motors stock. You also spend $50,000 and buy equity in land and a building that is leased to, and guaranteed by General Motors. Heaven forbid, General Motors starts down the tube into bankruptcy. Which of your two investments has less risk now? Obviously, the leased real estate. This is because as a general rule rents are paid first out of the remaining assets. Stockholders are paid last. Which, then, is the safer of the two investments? The leased real estate.

There are some forms of investments in real estate that can be and are, more risky than others. We should never play down this important fact. We will attempt, in this material, to help locate and identify and understand risk in a proposed real estate investment as we did with locating the Income Stream. The secret then is to learn the difference and be prepared for varying degrees of risk. Your desired yield rate, or IRR, then should reflect the degree of risk you are willing to take.

UNDERSTANDING THE RISK FACTORS

It is interesting to note that using the system of analysis of investment real estate discussed so far, you can now focus in on risk and identify it more clearly than ever before. Once it is identified you can determine the soundness of the investment by accumulating its risk factors and interpreting them into your own personal yield rate. Also, as you examine a property for its investment potential you may wish to readjust some particular risk factor to reflect a more conservative view, thereby lowering the price and reducing the risk.

Example:

An obvious risk factor in real estate investing is the vacancy rate of, say, an apartment complex. A buyer may or may not wish to accept the vacancy rate, as stated by the seller, which constitutes a portion of the risk he is taking. He then would simply adjust the rate to reflect his desired risk. This would be true of any of the many other "risk factors" inherent in real estate which we will discuss next.

THE INVESTMENT VARIABLES

To this point we have shown you some pretty positive ways to establish the value of an investment. On the basis of the soundness of this system it is reasonable to assume then that *if the numbers are correct the yields will be there*. However, there are assumptions and variables throughout this entire investment analysis process. This leads us to a conclusion that becomes a very important axiom in real estate investment analysis and that is:

1- IF THE NUMBERS ARE CORRECT THE
    YIELDS WILL BE THERE.

2- THE VARIABLES CONSTITUTE THE RISK.

3- UNDERSTAND THE VARIABLES AND YOU
    CAN COME VERY CLOSE TO CALCULATING
    THE RISK.

What are the variables? The variables are those items on the APOD, the CFA and the ACS worksheet that can fluctuate, (go up or down). These are the assumptions upon which the income stream is established and thereby a value determined.

VALUE PREDICATED ON THE FUTURE

It will be worthwhile for us to explore, at this juncture, a principle of value derivation that is not often comprehended. However, it will be important to you, as you go deeper into learning to establish value and understand risk.

Simply stated it says that

ALL VALUE IS PREDICTED UPON A FUTURE USE.

An appraisal of value of an income producing property, even though it is based upon past performance, is established on the premise that it will continue to earn or increase in value into the future.

You buy a stock or bond based on its past earnings yet its value to you is established according to its future earnings. You buy a lot, a diamond, some gold coins all on the premise that they will be worth more in the future. The market value or salability is predicated on this future rise in value or future earning power; otherwise it would not be salable to a rational investor.

LOCATING THE VARIABLES ON THE OFFERING DOCUMENTS

The profoundly significant part of our "new" system of

investment analysis is that while we are able to identify the elements of the income stream we can now also, for the most part, identify the risk areas. Keep in mind that the variables constitute the risk. Get a hold of the variables and you can understand the risk.

There are 7 major variables. (There may be other minor ones to consider with investor or property peculiarities.) There are three on the APOD statement, three on the CFA statement, and one on the ACS statement. They are described as follows:

VARIABLES OF THE APOD STATEMENT ARE:
1. The RENTS (line 1)
2. The VACANCY AND CREDIT LOSS (line 3)
3. The EXPENSES (lines 6-29)

VARIABLES OF THE CFA STATEMENT ARE:
1. The GROWTH FACTOR of the Potential Income & Expenses (lines 1 & 3)
2. The OPERATING EXPENSE PATTERN (line 7)
3. The TAX BRACKET of the owner (line 16)

VARIABLES OF THE ACS STATEMENT ARE:

1.   The PROJECTED SALES PRICE GROWTH
     FACTOR (top of form)

The list may appear at first to be voluminous and insurmountable. A close examination of each should reveal this is not so. Taken one at a time, examined and projected on a reasonable basis they can add stability to the soundness of the investment.

WHY ARE THE VARIABLES SUBJECT TO CHANGE?

The following discussion is a brief resume of why each item may not remain constant.

THE APOD VARIABLES

1- RENTS (Line 1)

The rent structure is a variable in that it can go up or down or be totally nonexistent. This variable is important to observe as it moves along in years, reflecting neighborhood changes, obsolescence, deterioration, lack of maintenance, economic trends and demands for the type of space offered.

2- VACANCY & CREDIT LOSS (Line 3)

All of the above is also true with this category. A miscalculation here can wipe out expected profits very quickly, particularly in a highly leveraged situation. An in-depth market study is important to establish a reasonable vacancy factor.

3- EXPENSES (Line 6 thru 29)

Every element of expense both actual and anticipated must be accounted for. Continued rises must be expected. A close efficient management must be maintained in order to keep a viable income stream which will in turn keep the value and the occupancy high.

(Let's take a brief sidestep and mention some temporary variables.)

TEMPORARY VARIABLES ON THE APOD UNTIL THE LOAN IS CLOSED AND PROPERTY TRANSFERRED

1- FINANCING (Top of APOD)

A. Assumption & Existing Loans

This can be a variable until absolute documentation can be obtained insuring the fact that existing loans are assumable, that the interest rates and all other terms and conditions remain the same, and that there will be no assumption fees required, no pay-off penalties, and no acceleration of the interest rate.

B. Potential Loans (Top of APOD)

This is also considered a variable until absolute documentation is finalized. The elevation of interest rates, reduction in loan amount, payment of points, etc. can seriously affect the whole statement, therefore, the yield.

2- CLOSING COSTS AND LOAN POINTS

While this is located as two separate items on the APOD statement, it should be included in the purchase price and equity required. It should always be stated as part of the equity even though much of it can be "expensed" out in the first year. It is considered a variable until the transfer is made due to the fact that the exact total amount required is not known until a few days before closing. Therefore, the total equity required could be misstated.

3- LAND TO IMPROVEMENT AND PERSONAL PROPERTY ALLOCATION (Top left of APOD)

This percentage of allocation of the purchase price distributed to each of these items is considered a variable until the depreciation schedule is established and accepted by the IRS. An upset can occur in the depreciation allowance until such an acceptance is made. This can affect the tax shelter hence the yield.

THE CFA VARIABLES

1. GROWTH FACTOR of the Potential Income & Vacancies (lines 1-3)

In order to determine the "appreciation value" portion of the income stream, a projection of growth in rents and therefore a growth in value needs to be made. As in the instance of establishing value in the appraisal process, past growth patterns are relied upon. The investor must look extremely close at this figure as it will have very significant impact upon the results.

2- OPERATING EXPENSES PATTERN (line 7)

This variable must be conservatively projected to allow escalation of taxes, insurance, labor, etc. and to allow for deterioration and the wearing out of the components required to maintain the income stream.

OTHER TEMPORARY VARIABLES (until Uncle Sam agrees with you)

1- COST RECOVERY SCHEDULE

(Depreciation - lines 11 and 12)

Though the options are very limited the depreciation schedule used on the offering documents may not be the final one selected after the investment has been transferred to the investor particularly as it applies to the breakdown of allocations given to land, buildings and improvements. It may also not be the one acceptable to the IRS. Therefore, this is an important variable.

2- TAX BRACKET OF THE OWNER (line 16)

The tax bracket used in the offering document is hypothetical and will probably not reflect the true tax situation of the new owner though it is somewhere close. Therefore, the prospective investor should, upon reviewing a property offering, insert his own tax bracket, being careful that the income and tax shelter received from the new investment include his own tax bracket computation. This should be done in consultation with his CPA.

THE ACS VARIABLES

1- PROJECTED SALES PRICE (Top of Form)

This is certainly a major variable in that it estimates what a Sale Price may be for the property at the end of the investment period. It is arrived at by using a cap rate that is consistent with current and anticipated market conditions. Various market influences such as inflation and an over or under supply of similar properties will have had an effect on the income stream during this period. With this, of course, is the aging of the property, deterioration, functional and economic obsolescence. These factors though, some negative, some positive, must be considered.

THE SUMMARY SHEET

A summary sheet enumerating the variables should always accompany the APOD, CFA, and ACS work sheets as part of the offering document.

Using the information from our sample property, a filled out Summary Sheet should look like this:

SUMMARY SHEET

Property __SAMPLE PROPERTY__   Date __Dec. 25,__ —

Summary of After-Tax Yields

Periods	Yields	
0	(40,000)	Original Investment
1	3,635	
2	4,386	
3	5,082	
4	5,810	
5	6,570 + 69,009	

__21.5__ % IRR

Summary of Variables Used

APOD		CFA	
1. Rents	39,120	1. Income Growth	5%
		2. Vacancy Pattern	5%
2. Vacancy & Credit Loss	5%	3. Expense Pattern STEADY AT	40.7%
3. Expenses	15,089	4. Tax Bracket of Owner	36%
	40.7%	ACS	
		1. Projected Sales Price	234,783
		2. Cap Rate Used	12%

EXHIBIT NO. 17

TO SUMMARIZE

In this segment we have discussed the fact that risk has a direct relationship with the projections or variables inserted into the investment analysis.

We have also arrived at certain conclusions:

1. **IF THE NUMBERS ARE CORRECT THE YIELDS WILL BE THERE.**

2. **THE VARIABLES CONSTITUTE THE RISK.**

3. **UNDERSTAND THE VARIABLES AND YOU CAN BEGIN TO ESTIMATE THE RISK.**

CHAPTER 10
THE INVESTMENT CURVES AND THE COMPUTER

WHEN TO SELL, EXCHANGE OR REFINANCE

Before we get into the topic of when to sell, exchange or refinance, it will be helpful to remind ourselves of a couple of unusual characteristics found in investment real estate.

It may startle you to know that the value we so often use and call the "appraised value" may not be the real value to you at all. In fact, chances are that it isn't. Why not? Simply because an appraisal of value must begin with, and be for, a stated purpose. Each purpose will have certain investment or ownership criteria around which a value is derived. The chances of those criteria exactly meeting your investment criteria, and tax situation, are a thousand to one shot. To illustrate, the following is a list of so-called "appraised values", each of which is correct and valid in its own context. However, each is different, initiated for a specific purpose, constructed around certain stipulated guidelines. Unless and until we get into the internal objectives of each appraisal they are of limited value to us. The first word describing the appraisal may give us some clue as to its purpose. Let's try it.

Economic value	Sale value
Stable value	Salvage value
Market value	Intrinsic value
Potential value	Extrinsic value
Book value	Tax value
Sound value	Rental value
Fair value	Speculative value
True value	Reproduction value
Depreciated value	Nuisance value
Warranted value	Liquidation value
Face value	Mortgage value
Cash value	Improved value
Capital value	Insurance value
Exchange value	Leasehold value

It becomes abundantly clear then that the "Appraised Value" is not the basis upon which we should invest. The reason being that we just do not know enough unless we are exposed to its inner workings. The two characteristics of real estate described below will further explain why.

In fairness to the so-called "Appraised Value" it is often just a rough guideline at best. It is used to reflect what other similar properties are being sold for, which would then tend to indicate only a range of value.

CHARACTERISTIC 1

DIFFERENT PEOPLE - DIFFERENT VALUE
SAME PROPERTY

A specific property can have one value to one person and an entirely different value to someone else. This is true because of income taxes.

As we have seen in the CFA form, the peculiarities of the tax bracket of the individual will greatly affect the annual CASH FLOW AFTER TAXES and the sales proceeds. In a heavy "tax shelter" type real estate investment, the higher the tax bracket of the owner the greater the yield-up to certain limits, of course. Therefore, the higher the value of the property to him.

On this premise then, it would appear that real estate investments are only for those who are in the upper tax brackets. This obviously is not true because we all have to pay taxes and can use some tax shelter however small. Not all real estate investments are good tax shelters. The message here is that each property must be examined on its own merits particularly as it relates to the investor's personal income tax situation.

CHARACTERISTIC 2
TODAY'S YIELD WILL NOT BE TOMORROW'S YIELD

One of the most fascinating things about real estate is that its yield elements are ever-moving, ever-changing, never constant. This is true not only in the field itself but for every individual property. There is within each property a continual fluctuation, a constant motion of its internal elements. On the surface this fact may strike fear in the hearts of some investors who seek the comfort of a constant yield. But when one learns why this is so, it can become an exciting challenge to finely tune each investment.

WHY THE MOVEMENT?

As the property matures or goes forward in time, its internal elements begin to move and are in continual motion throughout the investment life. Here are some of these elements and why they move. (The following is true of average properties and obviously not true of all situations.)

To illustrate, let's graphically display our Sample Property using the CFA worksheet, (Pages 56) and focus in on the CASH FLOW BEFORE TAXES, TAX LIABILITY and the CASH FLOW AFTER TAXES.

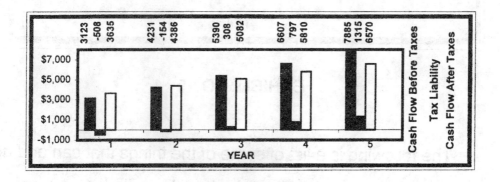

EXHIBIT NO. 18

Page 129

Now let's graphically plot the mortgage pay-down and the appreciation value as we did in our Horn of Plenty example .

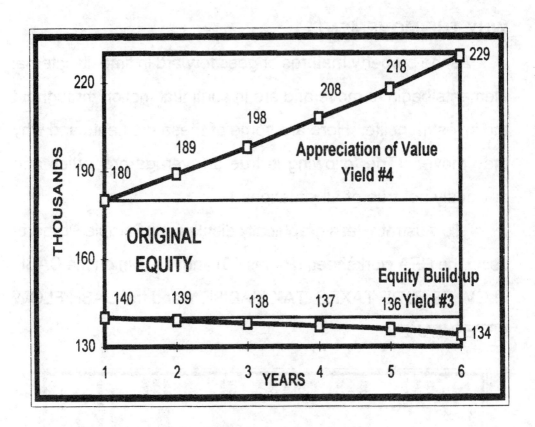

EXHIBIT NO 19

The following is a list of some of the things that can and do happen to investment real estate, together with the causes.

WHAT HAPPENS?	WHY?
A <u>T H E G R O S S OPERATING INCOME GOES UP OR DOWN</u>	Rents, generally, have risen due to inflation, and the increase in demand caused by population growth. When rents do not rise this tends to indicate that the property has peaked and is declining in value. When this occurs the investor must immediately review the property in light of the three investment decisions which follow.
B <u>THE EXPENSES GO UP</u>	There is hardly anyone who has not been affected by increased costs in nearly every cost of living segment. This, of course, is caused by inflation and has been true over the last 35 years. Because of this and because the property is getting older, expenses are continually rising.

C THE INTEREST PAYMENT GOES DOWN

As mortgage payments are made, the original loan amount is reduced. This means that less and less of the mortgage payment is applied to interest. Interest payments, therefore, go down as the mortgage is paid off.

D THE ORIGINAL TAX BASIS GOES DOWN

Tax basis is another way of saying original cost. As the property is depreciated down, an amount equal to the depreciation taken is subtracted from the original cost (or tax basis). This means that the capital gains liability realized at the time of sale is increased by a like amount.

E THE EQUITY GOES UP

This is the reverse of "C" above. As less and less of the mortgage payment goes toward interest, more and more is applied toward reducing the principal amount of the loan. As the loan balance is reduced the equity goes up.

F **THE TOTAL VALUE GOES UP**   As previously discussed, when inflation rises and demands grow, the price of real estate goes up.

These are just a few of the internal elements that are on the move. There are others but this should establish clearly that real estate yield components do continually move.

In ownership of investment real estate, it is important for us to understand that each movement alters the ownership benefits. Sometimes these alterations are positive. Sometimes they are negative. However, the aggregate or combined total of all the benefits, needs to be watched very closely. With the advent of the computer into the business of Real Estate Investment Analysis, this movement watching became very easy. This is particularly true if you are aware of the devices and techniques discussed so far in this book.

There will come a time when the total benefits of the property will begin to curve downward. This is because the equity in the building has grown. The Yield to Equity Ratio then gets smaller, producing 'lazy dollars'. At this point the investor must look at one of three investment alternatives available to him.

THE INVESTMENT ALTERNATIVES

Generally speaking there are three basic decisions to be made when a property's advantage begins to trend downward.

THEY ARE: 1.   KEEP THE PROPERTY.
             2.   SELL THE PROPERTY.
             3.   EXCHANGE THE PROPERTY.

Within each of these alternatives there are sub-alternatives which should be carefully reviewed.

THEY ARE: 1. KEEP THE PROPERTY.
                 a. Do nothing.
                 b. Refinance.
                 c. Upgrade the property.

d. Convert the property to another use.

2. <u>SELL THE PROPERTY.</u>
    a. Outright sale.
    b. Sell and leaseback.
    c. Sell with owner financing.

3. <u>EXCHANGE THE PROPERTY.</u>
    a. Outright exchange to a property of equal or higher value to achieve a "tax-deferred" status.
    b. Outright exchange to property of lesser value.

The big questions now are: "At what point on the 'Curve' does the aggregate of all my benefits rest? Which of the above investment alternatives is best for me under my present tax status?" These are important, even critical questions, the answers to which are vital to sound investment planning.

On the surface answering these questions may appear to be a very complicated process whereas in reality, if approached step by step, it is not. By now you should be familiar, at least, with the APOD, CFA and ACS forms. These forms, extended out or reversed to include previous years of ownership, will reveal the movement of certain internal elements within the investment.

To determine which of the above investment alternatives to use, however, does get a little more complicated. At this point you may wish to confer with your real estate investment counselor who is familiar with all we have discussed thus far. Certainly, those most qualified are the realtors who have the professional designation of CCIM. The CCIM designee is intensively trained and highly skilled in real estate investment analysis and tax-deferred exchanges. His designation is given by the National Association of Realtors (NAR) through the Commercial Investment Real Estate Institute (CIREI). His designation is comparable to that of MAI for appraisers, or CPA for accountants.

THE COMPUTER AND REAL ESTATE INVESTMENT ANALYSIS

The CCIM, or one similarly trained, will have available to him not only the forms and equipment previously discussed but probably access to up-to-date computer software. The latest computer programs have shown themselves to be invaluable in exploring investment alternatives. This is important because of the multiplicity of variables in every real estate investment that are continually changing, creating a variety of alternatives from which to select.

INTRODUCING THE FMRR AND THE INVESTMENT BASE CONCEPT

Before we discuss use of the computer it is important for us to understand some more basic criteria concerning the analysis of investment alternatives.

THE INVESTMENT BASE

To begin with let us consider the answer to the question, 'How do we handle the funds received periodically while we are waiting for them all to come in so that we might reinvest?' It will be necessary for us to determine exactly (or as closely as we can) what sum of money we will be dealing with. What is the aggregate of all the sums available for reinvestment? When determined, that amount of money plus any cash available is called the "Investment Base".

Another way to say "investment base" is the amount of cash and equity available for a new purchase or exchange. By starting with a single investment base the investor is able to compare alternatives more precisely. The investment base is arrived at by adding together all the yields gathered in to date, plus any new cash available and the fact that these yields, while awaiting to be reinvested are, at least, earning some interest.

THE FMRR

When this earned interest is combined with the IRR the yield rate is then called the "Financial Management Rate of Return" or the FMRR.

Stated another way, the FMRR is simply the IRR yields taken, when received, and placed in a savings account or some similar type liquid account, to collect interest until enough funds are gathered to go into another investment. The rate of interest applied to the projections usually coincides with existing bank rates. The rate then used is called "The Safe Rate".

A simplified example of converting the IRR into the FMRR using a Safe Rate of, say, 6% would be as follows:

Periods	Yields	ACCUMULATED CASH BALANCE
0	(12,000)	(END OF YEAR)
1	1,800	1,800
2	2,200	2,200 + 1,800 + (6% of 1800) = 4108
3	2,100	2,100 + 4,108 + (6% of 4108) = 6454
4	2,300	2,300 + 6,454 + (6% of 6454) = 9141
5	1,900	22,795 + 1900 + 9141 + (6% of 9141) = 34,384.
	+22,795	

27.44% IRR

TOTAL ACCUMULATED CASH EOY 5
PLUS 6% INTEREST = $34,384.

In order to arrive at the total accumulated income or the FMRR it is necessary to set up the "tee bar" as follows:

Periods	Yields	
0	(12,000)	
1	0	NOTE: The zeros are placed here because no
2	0	cash is being received rather it is out
3	0	earning 6% interest and is accumulating.
4	0	
5	34.384	TOTAL ACCUMULATED INCOME

23.43% FMRR

You will note that the FMRR is lower than the IRR figure. This is because the amounts received annually on the IRR analysis are yields directly to the original equity without anticipation of accumulation for reinvestment. The FMRR yields, however, are not received until the end of the investment life. During this time they have been accumulating and collecting interest at the current rate offered by an institution that stores cash and gives instant liquidity, a bank savings account, for example.

The "accumulation" process is necessary in order to establish the "investment base" (the amount of cash and equity available). Once the investment base is established we can go forward into our investment decisions and more accurately consider our alternatives.

A LOOK AT THE COMPUTER

With our understanding of FMRR and investment base we can now look at the computer and what it can do for us. Obviously we will have a myriad of numbers to go through, the slightest alteration to any one of which could change the net results. Therefore, the computer will be invaluable to us. Some real estate and investment professionals have already discovered the fact and have been using this marvelous device for some time.

COMPUTER SOFTWARE

In our search for the right computer software to match with NAR Forms we found many programs that did the job but then went well beyond the understanding level that we are striving for in THE INCOME STREAM.

These elaborate nuances are great and can be useful as you practice and gain further understanding of the analysis process. However, because they are not absolutely critical to achieve our goals let's put them aside for now.

Remember the premise of our objective........

The level of confidence in these systems is directly related to our understanding of the process.

To jump too far too fast will prove frustrating.

THE ROGER MARTIN CO.

Because of its wonderful simplicity and conformity with the NAR Forms we have selected the REA/L ESTATE ANALYSIS SOFTWARE from the Roger Martin Company of Tualatin, Oregon.

We feel that this software is as good as, or better than

most available today and at a price that is highly competitive in this field. By special permission this program is used to illustrate our sample property as follows. It is also used to further illustrate the software in Appendix B.

J. Roger Martin CCIM is the owner of the Roger Martin Co. and developer of the REA/L ESTATE ANALYSIS SOFTWARE. Roger is a true investment real estate professional whose career has spanned nearly 40 years. He achieved his CCIM designation in 1970, being the first in the state of Oregon. Since 1975 Roger has taught the Investment and Taxation segments of the REALTOR Institute program in many states plus many one-day tax seminars. He is currently active in dealing with and consulting with investors and REALTORS.

As an extra special bonus to readers of THE INCOME STREAM Roger Martin is offering the REA/L ESTATE ANALYSIS SOFTWARE at a deep discount in order to get you started. The software normally costs around $400 but the APOD and the CASHFLOW analysis of REA/L is available to you for only $49. (Order form Page 151. This offer is for a limited time and subject to change without notice.)

The
INCOME
STREAM

COMPUTER PRINTOUT

FOR

SAMPLE PROPERTY

REA/L ESTATE ANALYSIS SOFTWARE

EXHIBIT NO. 20

In reviewing the following problems, one should keep in mind that the tax laws are in a continual state of change. Therefore, the following material, as well as all the material in this book, should be viewed conceptually only. Answers to specific investment or tax questions should be sought from your CPA or Tax Attorney.

ANNUAL PROPERTY OPERATING DATA

Purpose	Sample Property	Date: Today
Name	Apartments	
Location	Anytown, USA	Notes:
Type Prop	10-Plex	

==

		Notes:
Price	180,000	
Loans	140,000	
Equity	40,000	

==

LOANS	Balance	Interest	Payment	Term	
1st	140,000	13.00	1,578.97	300.00	
2nd	0	0.00	0.00	0.00	
3rd	0	0.00	0.00	0.00	
Total	140,000		1,578.97	1.17	Debt Coverage Ratio

==

Assessed Values

			Notes:
Land	27,000	15.00%	
Improvement	153,000	85.00%	
Personal Prop.	0	0.00%	
Total	180,000	100.00%	

==

Potential Gross Income			39,120	4.60 GR
Plus: Other Income			0
Total Income			39,120
Less: Vacancy/Credit Loss (	5.00%)		1,956
Gross Operating Income			37,164

	- % -		Comments
Operating Expenses	0.00	0	
Accounting and Legal	1.09	425	
Advertise, Licenses, Permits	1.73	675	
Property Insurance	5.62	2,200	
Property Management	0.00	0	
Payroll - Resident Manager	4.60	1,800	
Other	0.00	0	
Workmens Comp	0.00	0	
Personal Property Taxes	0.00	0	
Real Estate Taxes	4.86	1,900	
Repairs and Maintenance	7.16	2,800	
Services - Elevator	0.00	0	
Janitorial	1.99	780	
Lawn	0.70	275	
Pool	0.00	0	
Rubbish	1.73	675	
Other	0.00	0	
Supplies	0.47	184	
Utilities- Electricity	3.07	1,200	
Gas and Oil	0.00	0	
Sewer and Water	4.60	1,800	
Telephone	0.96	375	
Other	0.00	0	
Miscellaneous	0.00	0	
	0.00	0	

TOTAL OPERATING EXPENSES		15,089
NET OPERATING INCOME	12.26% Cap Rate	22,075
Less: Total Annual Debt Service		18,948
CASH FLOW BEFORE TAXES	7.82% Cash on C.	3,127

REA/L SOFTWARE (C)Copyright 1988-98 J. Roger Martin, CCIM

Page 144

Purchase Price	180,000					
Initial Investment	40,000					

MORTGAGE DATA

LOAN BALANCES	Beginning Balance	Payments Per Year	Annual Interest	Monthly Payment	Remaining Term	Annual Total	Amortized Costs or Points
							0
1st Loan	140,000	12	13.00	1,578.97	300.00	18948	Total Amount to Amortize:
2nd Loan	0	12	0.00	0.00	0.00	0	0
3rd Loan	0	12	0.00	0.00	0.00	0	Amortize Over Years :

BALANCES (EOY) Year:	1998	1999	2000	2001	2002	2003	2004	2005	2006	2007
1st Loan End of Year	139,206	138,303	137,275	136,105	134,773	133,258	131,533	129,571	127,338	124,796
2nd Loan End of Year	0	0	0	0	0	0	0	0	0	0
3rd Loan End of Year	0	0	0	0	0	0	0	0	0	124,796
Totals	139,206	138,303	137,275	136,105	134,773	133,258	131,533	129,571	127,338	124,796
Principal Paid	794	903	1,028	1,170	1,332	1,515	1,724	1,962	2,233	2,542

TAXABLE INCOME

	1998	1999	2000	2001	2002	2003	2004	2005	2006	2007
POTENTIAL GROSS INCOME	39,120	41,076	43,130	45,286	47,551	49,928	52,425	55,046	57,798	60,688
+ Other Income	0	0	0	0	0	0	0	0	0	0
- Vacancy & Other Losses	1,956	2,054	2,156	2,264	2,378	2,496	2,621	2,752	2,890	3,034
GROSS OPERATING INCOME	37,164	39,022	40,973	43,022	45,173	47,432	49,803	52,293	54,908	57,654
- Operating Expenses	15,089	15,843	16,636	17,467	18,341	19,258	20,221	21,232	22,293	23,408
NET OPERATING INCOME	22,075	23,179	24,338	25,555	26,832	28,174	29,583	31,062	32,615	34,246
- Amortized Expenses	0	0	0	0	0	0	0	0	0	0
- Interest	18,154	18,044	17,920	17,778	17,616	17,432	17,223	16,985	16,714	16,406
- Depreciation	5332	5563	5563	5563	5563	5563	5563	5563	5563	5563
- Other Depreciation	0	0	0	0	0	0	0	0	0	0
- Participation	0	0	0	0	0	0	0	0	0	0
REAL EST. TAXABLE INCOME	(1,411)	(429)	855	2,214	3,653	5,178	6,796	8,514	10,337	12,277
- Loss Disallowed	0	0	0	0	0	0	0	0	0	0
Taxable This Year	(1,411)	(429)	855	2,214	3,653	5,178	6,796	8,514	10,337	12,277
LOSS CARRYFORWARD	0	0	0	0	0	0	0	0	0	0

CASH FLOWS

	1998	1999	2000	2001	2002	2003	2004	2005	2006	2007
Tax Bracket	36.00%	36.00%	36.00%	36.00%	36.00%	36.00%	36.00%	36.00%	36.00%	36.00%
NET OPERATING INCOME	22,075	23,179	24,338	25,555	26,832	28,174	29,583	31,062	32,615	34,246
- Annual Debt Service	18,948	18,948	18,948	18,948	18,948	18,948	18,948	18,948	18,948	18,948
- Capital Impr-Deprec.	0	0	0	0	0	0	0	0	0	0
- Capital Impr-Non Depr.	0	0	0	0	0	0	0	0	0	0
- Participation	0	0	0	0	0	0	0	0	0	0
CASH FLOW BEFORE TAXES	3,127	4,231	5,390	6,607	7,885	9,226	10,635	12,114	13,667	15,298
- Tax Liability	(508)	(154)	308	797	1,315	1,864	2,447	3,065	3,721	4,420
+ Tax Credits	0	0	0	0	0	0	0	0	0	0
CASH FLOW AFTER TAXES	3,635	4,385	5,082	5,810	6,570	7,362	8,188	9,049	9,946	10,878

PROCEEDS OF SALE

If Sold End of Year:	1998	1999	2000	2001	2002	2003	2004	2005	2006	2007
BEFORE TAX PROCEEDS	40,429	50,314	60,773	71,846	83,575	96,007	109,195	123,194	138,066	153,877
AFTER TAX PROCEEDS	39,038	45,867	53,049	60,750	69,009	77,867	87,372	97,573	108,526	120,293

	1998	1999	2000	2001	2002	2003	2004	2005	2006	2007
INTERNAL RATE OF RETURN	6.68%	16.72%	19.69%	20.93%	21.50%	21.77%	21.87%	21.88%	21.85%	21.78%
F.M.R.R.	6.68%	16.38%	18.82%	19.56%	19.69%	19.56%	19.30%	19.00%	18.68%	18.36%
Modified Initial Invest.	(40,000)	(40,000)	(40,000)	(40,000)	(40,000)	(40,000)	(40,000)	(40,000)	(40,000)	(40,000)
Accumulated Earnings	42,674	54,178	67,107	81,742	98,249	116,808	137,616	160,885	186,849	215,760

Safe Rate:	4.00%		Reinvestment Rate:		8.00%					

Page 145

SALE CALCULATION

ADJUSTED BASIS

	1998	1999	2000	2001	2002	2003	2004	2005	2006	2007
ORIGINAL BASIS	180,000	180,000	180,000	180,000	180,000	180,000	180,000	180,000	180,000	180,000
+ Capital Improvements	0	0	0	0	0	0	0	0	0	0
Sub-Total	180,000	180,000	180,000	180,000	180,000	180,000	180,000	180,000	180,000	180,000
- Depreciation	5,332	10,895	16,458	22,021	27,584	33,147	38,711	44,274	49,837	55,400
ADJUSTED BASIS AT SALE	174,668	169,105	163,542	157,979	152,416	146,853	141,289	135,726	130,163	124,600

GAIN ON SALE

	1998	1999	2000	2001	2002	2003	2004	2005	2006	2007
Sale Price	193,156	202,814	212,955	223,603	234,783	246,522	258,848	271,790	285,380	299,649
- Costs of Sale	13,521	14,197	14,907	15,652	16,435	17,257	18,119	19,025	19,977	20,975
- Adjusted Basis	174,668	169,105	163,542	157,979	152,416	146,853	141,289	135,726	130,163	124,600
- Participation	0	0	0	0	0	0	0	0	0	0
COST RECOVERY Recapture	-	10,895	16,458	22,021	27,584	33,147	38,711	44,274	49,837	55,400
CAPITAL GAIN	4,967	8,617	18,048	27,950	38,348	49,265	60,728	72,765	85,403	98,673

SUSPENDED LOSS CARRYFORWARD

	1998	1999	2000	2001	2002	2003	2004	2005	2006	2007
Capital Gain	4,967	8,617	18,048	27,950	38,348	49,265	60,728	72,765	85,403	98,673
- Loss Carryforward	0	0	0	0	0	0	0	0	0	0
TAXABLE GAIN	4,967	8,617	18,048	27,950	38,348	49,265	60,728	72,765	85,403	98,673

TAX LIABILITY ON SALE

		1998	1999	2000	2001	2002	2003	2004	2005	2006	2007
Tax Rate on Taxable Gain Yr 1	28%										
Unamortized Costs/Points		0	0	0	0	0	0	0	0	0	0
Tax on Unamortized Costs		0	0	0	0	0	0	0	0	0	0
Tax on Cost Recovery		-	2,724	4,115	5,505	6,896	8,287	9,678	11,068	12,459	13,850
Tax on Capital Gain - Year One	1,391		-	-	-	-	-	-	-	-	-
Tax on Capital Gain		-	1,723	3,610	5,590	7,670	9,853	12,146	14,553	17,081	19,735
Alternate Minimum Tax	0	0	0	0	0	0	0	0	0	0	0
TOTAL TAX LIABILITY		1,391	4,447	7,724	11,095	14,566	18,140	21,823	25,621	29,540	33,585

Rehabilitation tax credits may be subject to recapture

SALE PROCEEDS

	1998	1999	2000	2001	2002	2003	2004	2005	2006	2007
SALE PRICE	193,156	202,814	212,955	223,603	234,783	246,522	258,848	271,790	285,380	299,649
- Cost of Sale	13,521	14,197	14,907	15,652	16,435	17,257	18,119	19,025	19,977	20,975
- Loans	139,206	138,303	137,275	136,105	134,773	133,258	131,533	129,571	127,338	124,796
- Participation	0	0	0	0	0	0	0	0	0	0
PROCEEDS BEFORE TAX	40,429	50,314	60,773	71,846	83,575	96,007	109,195	123,194	138,066	153,877
- Tax Liability	1,391	4,447	7,724	11,095	14,566	18,140	21,823	25,621	29,540	33,585
PROCEEDS AFTER TAX	39,038	45,867	53,049	60,750	69,009	77,867	87,372	97,573	108,526	120,293

NET PRESENT VALUE

	1998	1999	2000	2001	2002	2003	2004	2005	2006	2007
APPROXIMATE N.P.V. AT: 12.00%	(1,899)	3,306	8,118	12,659	16,936	20,958	24,734	28,274	31,588	34,686
APPROXIMATE N.P.V. AT: 15.00%	(2,893)	1,159	4,699	7,874	10,715	13,252	15,513	17,521	19,301	20,875

INVESTMENT SUMMARY

Price	$	180,000
Total Loans		140,000
Loan to Value Ratio		77.78%
Initial Investment		40,000
Acquisition Fees		0
Total Annual Debt Service Year One		18,948
Annualized Loan constant		13.53
Debt Coverage Ratio		1.17
Gross Rent Multiplier		4.60
Potential Total Income		39,120
Vacancy and Operating Expenses		17,045
Net Operating Income		22,075
Capitalization Rate		12.26%
N.O.I. as Percent of Potential Total Income		56.43%
Cash Flow Before Taxes, 1st 12 months		3,127
Cash on Cash Percentage, 1st 12 months		7.82%
Approximate Tax Liability at tax rate of	36.00%	(508)
Cash Flow After Taxes, 1st 12 months		3,635
After Tax Cash on Cash, 1st 12 months		9.09%
Internal Rate of Return, End of Year Ten		21.78%
Financial Management Rate of Return		18.36%
Accumulated Wealth at End of Year Ten		215,760

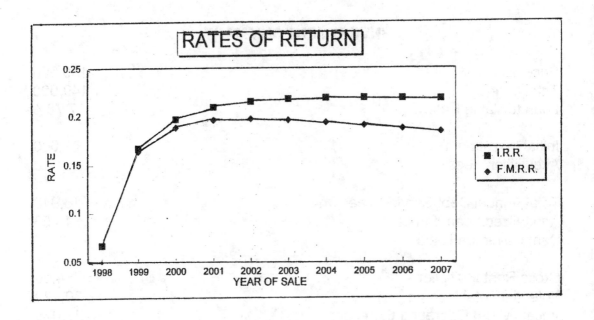

10 Year Cash Flows

n	$
0	(40,000)
1	3,635
2	4,385
3	5,082
4	5,810
5	6,570
6	7,362
7	8,188
8	9,049
9	9,946
10	131,171

21.78% I.R.R.
18.36% F.M.R.R.

Page 148

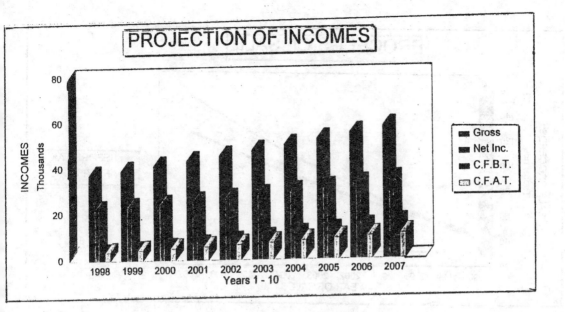

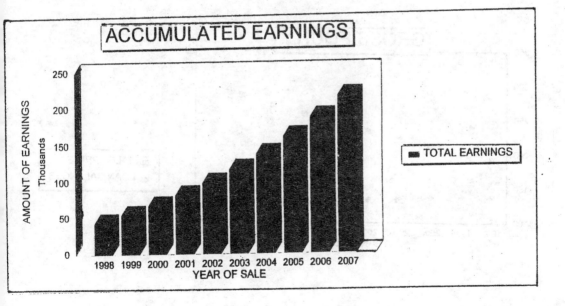

Page 149

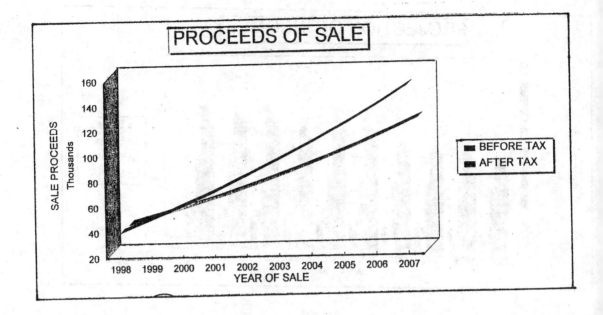

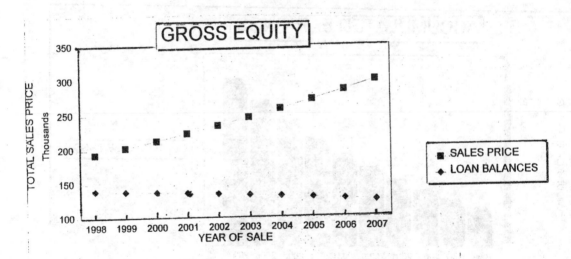

Exclusive special offer for purchaser's of

"The Income Stream"

REA/L ESTATE ANALYSIS SOFTWARE

REA/L Software
Order Form

Name_____

Company_____

PHONE ORDERS
With VISA or
MasterCard
(503) 682-2419

Address_____

City _____ State ___ Zip_____

$49 [ ] Lotus 1-2-3 Version 5.0 or higher

$49 [ ] Excel Version 5.0 or higher

Roger@RMartinCo.com
www.RmartinCo.com

P.O. Box 1148
Tualatin, OR 97062-1148

[ ] Check [ ] Visa/MasterCard

Expires _____

Card Number _____

Signature _____

(This offer for a limited time and subject to change without notice.)

CHAPTER 11

OWNERSHIP AND MANAGEMENT
OF INVESTMENT REAL ESTATE

Did you ever wonder who owns the barber shop on the corner or the strip shopping center down the street or the doctor's or dentist's office you visit occasionally? Would it surprise you to know that most of these buildings are not owned by the occupant at all but rather are owned by a landlord or investor like you.

Most businesses usually preserve their working capital for their business use and, therefore, elect to rent their space, the payments toward which are charged off as a business expense.

The market, the need, the demand is all around you. If you have a bit of courage and some understanding such as we have been offering so far in this book you should be looking into investment real estate. Assuredly it will take work and skill and patience but it will be well worth it.

We have attempted to present to you, so far, the basic techniques of real estate investment analysis. If you can get some understanding of it and find a good agent who also understands then you should begin inquiring. It is guaranteed to be interesting, exciting and fun. And, of course, highly profitable.

Now before you get started let me help you understand a very significant principle. It is called The Power of Leverage.

THE POWER OF LEVERAGE

Real estate because it is fixed and unique in nature enjoys the distinction of being the most mortgageable of all investment types. Because of this there is a powerful investment advantage available that many people fail to take into consideration. That advantage is leverage: The ability to borrow against an asset or use other peoples money. Here's an example:

Example:

Two identical properties are presented to two investors at the same time. The prices are $50,000 for each. They both buy. They keep their properties for a while and find that each has grown in value by 20%. Owner 'A' paid cash ($50,000) for his purchase.   Owner 'B' paid 20% down ($10,000) and mortgaged the balance.

How did the investments turn out so far?

	'A'	'B'
Down Payment	$50,000	$10,000
20% value increase	$10,000	$10,000
Yield Rate	20%	100%

Of course buyer 'B' had to make mortgage payments and pay interest, a portion of which is deductible from other income, and should be subtracted from his yield. But look at the difference because of the use of leverage.

Leverage can be a great thing when investing in real

estate but it can also be a curse depending on the amount and the terms of such financing. It's kinda' like fire: it can prepare you the best meal you ever had or it can burn your house down.

Wisdom is the watchword here.

BY WAY OF REVIEW - A REMINDER

Is it correct to look upon the IRR yield the same way as one would look upon an Interest Yield? Yes, it is, with one exception. The annual installment yields of the IRR may or may not, for that year, be equal to the overall IRR percentage rate. However, the yields are valid and will correctly reflect a return ON the investment as well as a return OF the investment. The investor needs to examine the "Tee-Bar" yields to see how their anticipated arrivals will match up with his own investment objectives.

How much IRR, or yield, is enough? Obviously, the yield or rate of return must first justify the risk taken, return the investment, and be equal to or better than market rates as viewed by the investor. Secondly, the yield should be adequate to cover anticipated inflation and any functional or economic obsolescence.

A METHOD TO ESTABLISH A DEBT COVERAGE RATIO

You may wish to see just how leveraged you are in an investment. Here is a simple way using the NOI and mortgage payment.

Using our sample property

YEAR	NOI with 5% Growth	Mortgage Payments	Debt Coverage Ratio
1	22,075	18,154	1.22
2	23,179	18,154	1.28
3	24,338	18,154	1.34
4	25,555	18,154	1.41
5	26,832	18,154	1.48

MANAGEMENT

Good, adequate, competent management is absolutely critical to the success of all real estate investments. In order for any cash-flow, controlled-expenses environment to work, management control must be in place. Remember that Income is our goal. Any dollar lost by not maximizing our cash flow or controlling our expenses comes directly off the bottom line. . . from your income and consequently the ultimate value of the property.

It has been wisely said that there are no bad managers... just bad owners. What is really being said is that if an owner pays a manager to take care of his property and then allows him to manage poorly the problem is obviously with the owner. If the manager does not do well the owner should be prepared to find another. Yes, we know, good management is hard to find but it is there if you are willing to communicate properly and compensate them adequately.

In this day and age of instant communication through mobile phones, fax machines, E-Mail, Internet and rapid-fire computers, there is little excuse for an owner not to be informed of the status of his investment. The real problem comes when an owner does not place enough importance on property management.

Here are some of the major mistakes that owners might make:

1- Failure to set up and maintain adequate management expense budgets,

2- Failure to set up reserves for repairs and replacements,

3- Failure to hire and use good professional managers,

4- Failure to spend money to maintain the integrity of the property and up-grade when needed,

5- Failure to keep informed.

Now, management may sound like a lot of work and hassle for the owner/investor which it can be if you let it get out of hand. Establishing clear criteria and expectations up front. Good management, yes, very good management is available if you seek it out and are willing to pay the price. Please make sure that you build it into your investment analysis.

A LITTLE WORD OF CAUTION

There are some rather crafty owners (or at least they would like for us to think them so) who will take a property and rape it for every last penny they can get from it. That is, do little or no maintenance, up grades or repair then place it on the market looking for what we call The Greater Fool. Greater Fool because it was very foolish to destroy the integrity of the property in the first place and he, the first fool, is now looking for a Greater Fool to buy it from him. We have driven home many times the necessity to examine first THE INCOME STREAM. We now say to you that **the second most important consideration of an income property is the condition of the buildings and their improvements.**

Our suggestion is that you examine carefully before you buy and walk away from properties being offered that have not been adequately maintained or else be prepared to pay for all those repairs that the previous owner still has in his pocket. The price should certainly reflect this if you do buy one of these properties.

A MANAGEMENT TIP

Among many of the top professional managers there is a saying that goes, "If you are 100% occupied you are not managing well." The substance of this is that you can never tell if your rents are at, or near, their highest rate until people decide . not to rent from you or go somewhere else because of price.

This of course is revealed by a small vacancy rate. Information which you will never have if you are always 100% occupied.

A SELLING TIP

As a seller you will want to be careful of the **'Wudjatake'** game played by some buyers that puts the seller at a disadvantage. It goes something like this:

Charlie has a horse for sale. The price is $1,500. Sam, a prospective buyer, approaches and asks, "WUDJATAKE $1,200 FOR THE HORSE?". Charlie pauses for a moment then says "Well, yeah, if that's the best you can do". Whereupon Sam starts to be critical of some of the lesser points of the animal and asks, "WUDJATAKE $1,000 FOR THE HORSE?." Charlie, after listening to this negative sales pitch and realizing what a poor animal he has had all this time , finally succumbs and says, "Yeah, well OK". Then Sam really moves in for the kill

After a very close examination from nose to tail, examining the teeth, the hooves, legs and underbelly he finally asks, "WUDJATAKE $900 FOR THE HORSE? THAT'S THE VERY BEST I CAN DO."

We're not sure what Sam's answer was, depending on how badly he wanted to get rid of the horse, but the point has been made. The principle here is that when Sam made the offer he only committed Charlie not himself. Charlie's first reply should have been, "Are you making that as a firm offer?"

The thing we learn from this is that when offers come in on your property they should ALWAYS be in writing with an earnest money deposit. Some crafty buyers will try to get around that by putting a lot of conditions in an offer to buy. It is best to get ALL the conditions worked out before you give an answer to that wonderful question WUDJATAKE.

Another answer that might be given to a buyer who is obviously trying to get a bargain, assuming that the property is fairly priced in the beginning and the seller has no urgency, is "I want to wait 30 days to see how it goes before I consider any price reductions."

CHAPTER 12

HOW TO ANALYZE YIELDS FROM OTHER INVESTMENTS

Other Investments - How to Value their income streams

Comes now one of the real rewards and advantages of your diligence so far in your study of this material. If you understand the principles previously discussed, you now have the ability to analyze the real return of any investment.

The reason we need to analyze is because real yields and real values are hard to see without it. To graphically illustrate that things aren't always as they seem, we offer the following Alternative Investment Comparison chart . (This is something that we have been using for the last 30 years and are not sure of its original source but it makes a point.)

Suppose that the cash payments received as shown

below represent the after-tax cash flows from the alternative investments as indicated. Further, suppose that each of the investments requires a $10,000 initial capital investment. If you, as an investor, had only $10,000 to invest, which one of the five available would you pick?

End of Year	Mortgage Purchased at a Discount	Purchase of a 5 year Note	Stock Purchase	Insurance Annuity	Land Purchase
1	$1,627.45	0	$1,000.00	$1,000.00	0
2	1,627.45	0	1,000.00	Each	0
3	1,627.45	0	1,000.00	Year	0
4	1,627.45	0	1,000.00	To	0
5	1,627.45	16,105.10	1,000.00	Perpetuity	0
6	1,627.45	0	1,000.00		0
7	1,627.45	0	1,000.00		0
8	1,627.45	0	1,000.00		0
9	1,627.45	0	1,000.00		0
10	1,627.45	0	11,000.00		25,937.42
Total Receipts	$16,274.50	$16,105.10	$20,000.00		$25,937.42

EXHIBIT NO. 22

When the above examples are discounted to meet a time value of money, we find that they are all yield the same return. Each produces a 10% rate of return.

Let's consider a few other examples and show how exciting this understanding can be.

Remember the rule that in order for any investment type to be considered on an equal basis, the yields must be clearly identified. These yields must be stated "after" income taxes and "after" sales and/or transfer costs.

Suppose you suddenly inherit $25,000 in cash. You know that stationary money in an inflationary economy is a guaranteed loss. Therefore, you enter the marketplace to invest. There are many people out there eager to take your money. Each is touting his investment to be the best. At this point you begin to remember all those important investment criteria that must be considered. These are what we know as "The Significant Six":

     1- Risk (How safe is my principal?)

2- Liquidity (How quickly can I convert to cash?)

3- Tax consequences (How much will 'Uncle Sam' take?)

4- Growth potential (Will the value of the investment grow and keep up with, or exceed, inflation?)

5- Yield factors (Is this the highest possible return I can get and will it compensate for all of the above?)

6- Management (How much time and effort do I need to spend in behalf of this investment?)

These are the 6 most significant questions that an investor can ask in any investment situation. They all should be looked into very carefully.

There are some people who will take just about any risk if the yields are high enough. This, of course, depends upon their temperament and financial ability to take a loss if necessary. As an individual you must decide these things for yourself before you go into the market. You must assure yourself that the yield will justify the risk. Many will pursue a course of <u>investment</u>

<u>diversification - a balancing of the investment portfolio</u>: Some high risk investments, some low risk investments. This is a wise and correct principle of investing.

EXAMPLES:

You now have FIVE different investment opportunities in front of you:

1- Gold

2- Stock

3- Mortgage

4- Land

5- Tax Free Bond

Each is different in its own way. You suddenly recall a few investment rules like "The value of an investment is established according to its income stream" or "All other considerations are important, but only as they strengthen or enhance the income stream." Your job now is to identify and valuate each income stream for it's REAL income. Recognizing the importance of this, you gather the following information on the proposed investments and lay them out. (Let's suppose you are in the 40% tax bracket)

Example 1- Gold.

You buy $25,000 worth of Gold Kruegerands at today's price which is $459 per ounce. The handling or acquisition costs are 9% or $41 per ounce. You buy 50 ounces for your $25,000. You keep the gold for five years and find the value has risen to $750 per ounce. You sell and pay the capital gains taxes which are $2000. Your net proceeds are $35,500. To determine your REAL yield, set up the "Tee" bar and find the annual rate of return.

Periods	Yields	
0	(25,000)	Purchase Price
1	0	
2	0	**7.26% Annual Yield**
3	0	
4	0	
5	35,500	Net Sales Price

Example 2- Stock

A good stock is offered to you that has an anticipated 5% annual dividend and is appreciating at the rate of 10% a year. You invest the $25,000 and receive a 5% annual dividend of $1250 out of which you must pay capital gains tax after the exclusion exemption of $168. Therefore, your annual dividend nets out at $882. At the end of 5 years you decide to sell. You find that the stock did indeed grow at the rate of 10% per year. Your value at sale then is $40,263. Out of this you are required to pay approximately $2,442 in capital gains taxes. Sales charges are $1,135. Your net sales proceeds are $36,686. Graphically it will look like this:

Periods	Yields	
0	(25,000)	
1	882	
2	882	**11.03% Annual Yield**
3	882	
4	882	
5	882	+ 36,686

Example 3- Mortgage

You are offered a $25,000 mortgage on a good commercial building. It will pay you 13% annually for a period of 7 years. The annual payments are $5652.77. The interest you receive is taxed as ordinary income; therefore, your annual proceeds would be as follows:

Yr	Receive	Interest	Principal	Taxes	Income After Tax Income
1	5652.77	3250.00	2402.77	1300.00	4352.77
2	5652.77	2937.64	2715.13	1175.06	4477.71
3	5652.77	2584.67	3068.10	1033.87	4618.90
4	5652.77	2185.82	3466.95	874.33	4778.40
5	5652.77	1735.12	3917.65	694.05	4958.72
6	5652.77	1225.82	4426.95	490.33	5162.44
7	5652.77	650.32	5002.45	260.13	5392.64

Arranged on the "Tee" bar your mortgage yield would be:

Periods	Yields	
0	(25,000)	
1	4352.77	
2	4472.71	**7.8% Annual Yield**
3	4618.90	
4	4778.40	
5	4958.72	
6	5162.44	
7	5392.64	

Example 4- Land

A good land investment is available for $25,000 (no mortgage). It looks good and should double your money in 5 years. The property taxes, liability insurance and periodical mowing costs equal $550 per year. Assuming the property taxes, insurance and mowing costs are expensed against ordinary income, the approximate net cost per year would be $330. Structured on the "Tee" bar it should look like this.

Periods	Yields	
0	(25,000)	
2	(330)	
3	(330)	**13.85% Annual Yield**
4	(330)	
5	(330) + 50,000	

Example 5- Bond - Tax Free Municipal

Your city is offering some municipal bonds. It's a solid, progressive town and you want to invest in it. The bonds will bear 8% and are free from income taxes. Assume the market stays strong for the next 5 years and they are redeemable at that time for face value. It would appear graphically this way:

Period	Yields
0	(25,000)
1	2,000
2	2,000 **8.0% Annual Yield**
3	2,000
4	2,000
5	2,000 + 25,000

RECAPITULATION

On the surface there appears to be something strange about this whole thing. How is it that (1) the Gold purchase, which grew at a rate of 50% in five years (10% per year) only showed a 7.26% annual yield rate; or (2) the stock purchase which yielded 5% annually and appreciated at 10% per year only yielded a 11.03% annually; and why is it that (3) the mortgage which was at a fixed interest rate of 13% only showed a 7.8% annual yield; or how come (4) the land which grew by 100% in five years only yielded 14.19% annually? Only the tax exempt bond which contracted to yield 8% actually did yield 8%.

It should be pretty obvious by now that there are many external forces affecting our investments which we often fail to take into consideration. We must always plan out our investments, lay out the yields, and examine the income streams for what they really are. We must always consider expenses, such as operating costs, taxes, insurance, acquisition costs, sales costs and, above all, our personal tax status as it applies to any particular investment. Needless to say, had your hypothetical tax bracket been higher or lower than the projected 40% the results would have been much different in every instance except the tax free bond.

Savings Accounts and Life Insurance

There are a couple of other places wherein we place our money in great quantities that are not really considered to be investments but, because so much of your hard-earned dollars goes into these areas, it is worth the space to explain what the yield consequences could be. These two areas are (1) savings accounts (to include Certificate of Deposits and Money Market Certificates) and (2) "whole-life" life insurance. Here are a couple of examples:

Example 1- Savings Accounts

You take $10,000 of your money and place it in a savings account which bears 6% interest. You leave it in for 5 years and let it compound itself. At the end of 5 years you have a total of $13,382.26 in the bank. The earned interest of $3,382.26 is subject to ordinary income tax. Your rate of 40% is applied thus leaving you a total gain of $2,029.36. At the end of 5 years your net balance is $12,029.36. Your "real" annual yield is:

Period	Yields
0	(10,000)
1	0
2	0
3	0
4	0
5	12,029

3.76% Annual Yield

Example 2- "Whole life" life insurance

Suppose for protection against an untimely death you consider life insurance. Life insurance gives you an "Instant" estate which upon your death will provide for your family. However, you have a good agent who likes to make money and he sells you on the idea of taking a "whole life" policy which not only provides you with an instant sum of money upon death (protection) but one that would also include a "cash value" income (retirement plan) after a stipulated period of time. A forced savings, so to speak, which would earn you a yield while the insurance company had it. So you consider a $100,000 whole-life policy. You are age 38 therefore your annual premium would be $1,905. The policy agrees to give you protection and to pay you either $54,600 at age 58 or $95,000 at age 65. The protection side of the policy will cancel when the "cash value" is received. You are on your own from this point forward. Your 'Instant Estate' is now reduced to only the cash value. (That's just as well, you're getting too old for them to insure you anyway. Or was it planned that way?) In order to accurately compute the amount of money being earned on your money going into the "cash value" account we will have to make the following computation:

If you had taken only the protection side of the policy (term insurance), your annual cost may have been approximately $925 per year. Subtract this amount from the $1,905 and the remainder is that portion which is used for the "cash value" account. This amount would be $980. Structured on the "Tee" bar your payments applied to the "cash value" receivable looks like this:

Cash-Out at age 58		Cash-Out at age 65	
Period	Yields	Period	Yields
0	(980)	0	(980)
1	(980)	1	(980)
2	(980)	2	(980)
3	(980)	3	(980)
	(980)		(980)
20	(980) + 54,600	27	(980) + 95,100
8.99% Annual Yield		**8.17% Annual Yield**	

NOTE 1. There is a payment made at "0" because premiums are paid in advance.

2. There will be income taxes due at the ordinary income rate on the interest earned. However, we made no allowance for this in the example due to the fact that the tax bracket of the policy holder would probably be seriously reduced by this time.

You will notice the absence of an example of investment real estate. There are adequate examples in the preceding chapters. It was not our purpose to show the superiority of one sort of investment over another. Rather, it was to show you the difference between these various investment types. They can all be brought together with a common denominator: the interest rate, the IRR, the FMRR, the Annual Yield or whatever you choose to call it. It is clearly what the investment is earning.

It should also be imminently clear that each investment needs to be looked into thoroughly to understand what the real yield really is. It should also be abundantly clear that each investment MUST be looked into to determine how it affects your own personal income tax situation.

When considering an investment, look at the INCOME STREAM. If you do this with diligence we won't have to say another word about real estate as an investment. It will simply speak for itself.

The
INCOME
STREAM

APPENDIX A

BLANK ANALYSIS FORMS

APOD
CFA
ACS
SUMMARY SHEET

Annual Property Operating Data

Name _____

Location _____

Type of Property _____

Size of Property _____ (Sq. Ft./Units)

Purpose _____

Purchase Price _____

Acquisition Costs _____

Loan Points _____

Down Payment _____

Assessed/Appraised Values		Existing	Balance	Payment	#Pmts. /Yr.	nterest	Term
Land	____ ____	1st	____	____	12	____	____
Improvements	____ ____	2nd	____	____	12	____	____
Personal Property	____ ____						
Total	____	Potential					
		1st	____	____	____	____	____
Adjusted Basis as of:	____	2nd	____	____	____	____	____

	$/SQ FT or $/Unit	% of GOI		COMMENTS/FOOTNOTES
ALL FIGURES ARE ANNUAL				
1 POTENTIAL RENTAL INCOME	____			
2 Plus: Other Income (affected by vacancy)				
3 Less: Vacancy & Cr. Losses	(	0 ____)		
4 EFFECTIVE RENTAL INCOME				
5 Plus: Other Income (not affected by vacancy)				
6 GROSS OPERATING INCOME	____			
OPERATING EXPENSES:				
7 Real Estate Taxes	____	____		
8 Personal Property Taxes	____	____		
9 Property Insurance	____	____		
10 Off Site Management	____	____		
11 Payroll	____	____		
12 Expenses/Benefits	____	____		
13 Taxes/Worker's Compensation	____	____		
14 Repairs and Maintenance	____	____		
Utilities:				
15 _____	____	____		
16	____	____		
17	____	____		
18	____	____		
19 Accounting and Legal	____	____		
20 Licenses/Permits	____	____		
21 Advertising	____	____		
22 Supplies	____	____		
23 Miscellaneous Contract Services:	____	____		
24	____	____		
25	____	____		
26	____	____		
27	____	____		
28				
29 TOTAL OPERATING EXPENSES	____	____		
30 NET OPERATING INCOME	____	____		
31 Less: Annual Debt Service				
32 Less: Funded Reserves				
33 Less: Leasing Commissions	____	____		
34 Less: Capital Additions	____	____		
35 CASH FLOW BEFORE TAXES	____	____		

Prepared by: _____

Cash Flow Analysis Worksheet

Property Name	_____		Purchase Price	_____
Prepared For	_____		Acquisition Costs	_____
Prepared By	_____		Loan Points	_____
Date Prepared	8-May-98		Down Payment	_____

Mortgage Data			Cost Recovery Data		
	1st Mortgage	2nd Mortgage		Improvements	Personal Property
Amount			Value		
Interest Rate			C. R. Method	SL	
Term			Useful Life		
Payments/Year	12	12	In Service Date		
Periodic Payment	-	-	Recapture		
Annual Debt Service	-	-	(All/None/Excess)		
Comments			Investment Tax Credit ($$ or %)		

Taxable Income

Year :					
1 Potential Rental Income					
2 +Other Income affected by vacancy					
3 -Vacancy & Credit Losses					
4 =Effective Rental Income					
5 +Other Income not affected by vacancy					
6 =Gross Operating Income					
7 -Operating Expenses					
8 =NET OPERATING INCOME					
9 -Interest - 1st Mortgage					
10 -Interest - 2nd Mortgage					
-Cost Recovery - Improvements					
12 -Cost Recovery - Personal Property					
13 - _____					
14 - _____					
15 =Real Estate Taxable Income					
16 Tax Liability @ _____ (Savings)					

Cash Flows

17 NET OPERATING INCOME (Line 8)					
18 -Annual Debt Service					
19 - _____					
20 - _____					
21 =CASH FLOW BEFORE TAXES					
22 -Tax Liability (Savings) (Line 16)					
23 +Investment Tax Credit					
24 =CASH FLOW AFTER TAXES					

Alternative Cash Sales Worksheet

Mortgage Balances

	Year:				
Principal Balance - 1st Mortgage					
Principal Balance - 2nd Mortgage					
TOTAL UNPAID BALANCE					

Calculation of Sale Proceeds

PROJECTED SALES PRICE

CALCULATION OF ADJUSTED BASIS:
1   Basis at Acquisition
2   + Capital Additions
3   - Cost Recovery (Depreciation) Taken
4   - Basis in Partial Sales
5   =Adjusted Basis at Sale

CALCULATION OF EXCESS COST RECOVERY
6   Total Cost Recovery Taken (Line 3)
7   - Straight Line Cost Recovery
8   =Excess Cost Recovery

CALCULATION OF CAPITAL GAIN ON SALE:
9   Sale Price
10   - Costs of Sale
11   - Adjusted Basis at Sale (Line 5)
12   - Participation Payments
13   =Total Gain
14   - Excess Cost Recovery (Line 8)
15   - Suspended Losses
16   =Gain or (Loss)
17   - Straight Line Cost Recovery (limited to gain)
18   =Capital Gain from Appreciation

ITEMS TAXED AS ORDINARY INCOME:
19   Excess Cost Recovery (Line 8)
20   - Unamortized Loan Points
21   =Ordinary Taxable Income

CALCULATION OF SALE PROCEEDS AFTER TAXES:
22   Sale Price
23   - Cost of Sale
24   - Participation Payments
25   - Mortgage Balance(s)
26   =Sale Proceeds Before Tax
27   - Tax (Savings) Ordinary Income at ____% (Line21)
28   - Tax on Straight Line Recapture at ____% (Line 17)
29   - Tax on Capital Gains at ____% (Line 18)
30   =Sales Proceeds After Taxes

SUMMARY SHEET

Property _____   Date _____

Periods	Yields
0	(_____) Original Investment
1	_____
2	_____
3	_____
4	_____
5	_____
	_____
	_____
	_____
	_____
	_____
	_____

_____ % IRR

Summary of Variables Used

APOD	CFA
1. Rents	1. Income Growth
	2. Vacancy Pattern
2. Vacancy & Credit Loss	3. Expense Pattern
3. Expenses	4. Tax Bracket of Owner
	ACS
	1. Projected Sales Price
	2. Cap Rate Used

Remarks: _____

_____

Prepared by: _____

The statements and figures presented herein, while not guaranteed, are secured from
BG SS-1   sources we believe authoritative.

The
INCOME
STREAM

APPENDIX B

REA/L ESTATE ANALYSIS SOFTWARE

INFORMATION

REA/L ESTATE ANALYSIS SOFTWARE

CASH FLOW ANALYSIS FORMS

The **APODCF** worksheet starts with an operating statement for the loan information, income and expenses. That information is the basis for a cash flow projection.

Recent Tax Acts have complicated the lives of ever REALTOR, investor, CCIM and CPA in the business. To create an accurate cash flow analysis, you have to keep track of active/passive status, the investor's Adjusted Gross Income, tax brackets, etc.

The REA/L cashflow analysis **"knows"** things like:
- Current tax tables.
- How to treat taxable income, depending on whether the investor is active, passive or someone in the real estate business.
- How to handle the $25,000 exclusion.
- How to phase out between $100,000 and $150,000 Adjusted Gross Income.
- How to reduce the rate if the profit in the sale year pushes the investor beyone the maximum capital gains tax level.

In short, the worksheet "thinks" like a CCIM because it was created by one! You just plug in the data and the worksheet crunches out a complete and accurate 10-year cash flow analysis.

The **input-screen** pictured above offers a number of flexible options. **You can change:**
- Adjusted Gross Income from year to year. Or, if you enter only the first year, it assumes the same figure for years 2 - 10.
- Growth rates on the income and expense items. You enter the first year, and it does the rest. There is also a **manual-input** screen so you can manually enter the income and expenses for each year.
- Choices for calculation of Sale Price
- Loan section inputs for loan fees and other costs to amortize.
- Capital improvements from year to year.
- Built-in tax tables or manual input.
- Cost recovery methods and improvement allocation

Once the operating statement is complete, the input screens might take a minute or two. At that time, the cash flow analysis pictured **is already competel** For times when you don't need an operating statement, there is a **fast-input** screen where you can actually create a 10-year cash flow analysis in under 2 minutes **TOTAL**.

The Internal Rate of Return & the Financial Management Rate of Return are calculated as-if it were sold each at the end of **each year**.

Samples at: http://www.teleport.com/~jrmartin

Roger Martin Company
P. O. Box 1148
Tualatin, OR 97062-1148
(503) 682-2419 - jrmartin@teleport.com

REA/L ESTATE ANALYSIS SOFTWARE

OPERATING STATEMENTS

You do these computations all the time. Now you can do them **FAST** and **EASY**.

REA/L contains several different operating statements like those used in GRI and CCIM courses all over the country. Like all REA/L worksheets, change input and instantly see the results.

You work **directly on forms** you're already familiar with, while the computer works in the background to perform the calculations.

There are **no complex menus to master**. You don't have to know much about computers or spreadsheets to be "up and running" REA/L Software within the first hour.

All the forms pictured actually appear directly on the screen. You simply move around and plug numbers in the input areas.

The loan section of the form lets you quickly find the remaining term on a loan, or find a payment if you already know the term.

Change a balance, see the payment. Change income, see the new cap rate. **All changes recalculate immediately**.

Playing "what-if" couldn't be easier!

Beyond a standard single-column operating statement, another statement has two columns. You can include last year and a projection side by side. Have a different expense item than those listed? Change it. All expense items can be modified to fit the property.

The APOD-5 is an operating statement with 5 columns for an extremely detailed projection. Or use it to create several different scenarios side by side. Need more than 5 columns? APOD-10 is the answer!

When you want to start with some historical income and expense data, one of the operating statements starts with a page looking like an IRS Schedule "E". Key in the data from last years "E" and the income/expense data is automatically transferred to a double-column operating statement.

REA/L's **flexibility** allows you to make modifications to fit your needs.

Samples at: http://www.teleport.com/~jrmartin

Roger Martin Company
P. O. Box 1148
Tualatin, OR 97062-1148

(503) 682-2419 - jrmartin@teleport.com

ANNUAL PROPERTY OPERATING DATA

				Date	
Purpose	Example				
Name	Testime		Notes		
Location	Wherever U R				
Type Prop	Courtyard Apts				

		Notes
Price	650,000	
Loans	400,000	
Equity	250,000	

LOANS	Balance	Interest	Payment	Term	Comments:
1st	400,000	9.00	-3218.49	350.00	
2nd			0.00		
3rd			0.00		
Total	400,000		3218.48		

Assessed Values			Notes
Land	120,000	22.02%	
Improvement	425,000	77.98%	
Personal Prop.	0	0.00%	
Total	545,000	100.00%	

Gross Scheduled Income			95,000	97,500
Plus: Other Income			2,400	3,000
Total Income			97,400	100,500
Less: Vacancy/Credit Loss	5.13%	4.83%	5,000	4,850
Gross Operating Income			92,400	95,850

LESS: Operating Expenses				
Accounting and Legal			150	150
Advertising, Licenses, Permits			265	
Property Insurance			1,810	1,810
Property Management			4,620	5,739
Payroll - Resident Manager			0	0
Other			0	0
Taxes-Workmens Comp.			0	0
Personal Property Taxes			0	0
Real Estate Taxes			12,000	12,500
Repairs and Maintenance			3,540	4,000
Services - Elevator			0	0
Janitorial			1,300	1,500
Lawn			360	360
Pool			0	0
Rubbish			1,345	1,345
Other			0	0
Supplies			0	0
Utilities- Electricity			180	180
Gas and Oil			0	0
Sewer and Water			1,150	1,150
Telephone			195	195
Other			0	0
Miscellaneous			500	600
			0	0
TOTAL OPERATING EXPENSES			27,275	29,829
NET OPERATING INCOME	10.02%	10.11%	65,125	65,721
Less: Total Annual Debt Service			38,622	38,622
CASH FLOW BEFORE TAX	10.60%	10.84%	26,503	27,099

Purpose	Reconstructed				
Address	1234 Overthere				
City/State	Wherever U R				
Type Prop.	Courtyard Apts				

Price	650,000	
Loans	400,000	
Equity	250,000	

LOANS	Balance	Interest	Payment	Term
1st	400,000	8.00	-3001.70	330.00
2nd			0.00	
3rd			0.00	
Total	400,000		3001.70	

		Column 1
Debt Coverage Ratio		1.81
Annual Loan Constant		9.01%
Loan to Value Ratio		61.54%
Equity to Value Ratio		38.46%
Gross Rent Multiplier		6.84
Net Income % of Gross		66.84%
Capitalization Rate		10.03%
Cash on Cash Percents		11.67%

Assessed Values			Notes:
Land	120,000	22.02%	
Improvement	425,800	77.98%	
Personal Prop	0	0.00%	
Total	545,800	100.00%	

Operating Statement	1994	Adjusted	1995	Adjusted	Projection
Gross Scheduled Income	97,850	97,850	110,131	110,131	123,953
Plus: Other Income	2,472	2,472	2,782	2,782	3,131
Total Income	100,322	100,322	112,913	112,913	127,084
Less: Vacancy/Credit Loss	5,150	5,150	5,797	5,797	6,525
Gross Operating Income	95,172	95,172	107,116	107,116	120,559

Less: Operating Expenses					
Accounting and Legal	150	150	150	150	150
Advertising, Licenses, Permits	265	265	265	265	265
Property Insurance	1,810	1,810	1,810	1,810	1,610
Property Management	4,620	4,620	4,620	4,620	4,620
Payroll - Resident Management					
Other					
Taxes-Workmens Comp					
Personal Property Taxes					
Real Estate Taxes	12,750	14,250	15,750	17,250	18,750
Repairs and Maintenance	3,540	3,540	3,540	3,540	3,540
Services - Elevator					
Janitorial	1,300	1,300	1,300	1,300	1,300
Lawn	360	360	360	360	360
Pool					
Rubbish	1,345	1,345	1,345	1,345	1,345
Other					
Supplies					
Utilities- Electricity	180	180	180	180	180
Gas and Oil					
Sewer and Water	1,150	1,150	1,150	1,150	1,150
Telephone	195	195	195	195	195
Other					
Miscellaneous	2,500	500	3,000	500	600
TOTAL OPERATING EXPENSES	29,965	29,465	33,465	32,465	34,085
NET OPERATING INCOME	65,207	65,707	73,651	74,651	86,494
Less: Total Annual Debt Service	36,020	36,020	36,020	36,020	36,020
CASH FLOW BEFORE TAXES	29,187	29,687	37,631	38,631	50,474

REA/L ESTATE ANALYSIS SOFTWARE

SALE CALCULATIONS

Once the operating statement and input information is complete, the cash flow analysis projection and the sale calculations are automatically completed. Rather than just calculating a sale at the end of the projection time, REA/L determines what the results would be AS-IF it were sold at the end of each year. The printout to the right is of the potential sales.

The cash flow analysis also includes the pictured summary. There's blank room at the end of the page if you want to add something else ... like a disclaimer!

Another feature on the cash flow, is a buy versus lease analysis. After completing a purchase scenario, add lease information for a comparison.

REA/L Software is programmed with menus for all the functions you regularly need. To print, bring up the menu and tap the letter P or click the choice with your friendly rodent. To clear the worksheet, tap C. **Efficient and easy to use!**

Time tests revealed you can create a complete cashflow analysis in less than 1/3 of the time of software costing three times more. REA/L saves you money now, and time from from here to eternity!

A CCIM said **"It's like magic. . . a miracle!"**
A CCIM instructor said **"REA/L is the only software I'd ever recommend!"**

There are **five graphs** on the cash flow analysis.
- Incomes (Gross, Net, Cash flow before and after tax)
- Internal Rate of Return and F.M.R.R.
- Gross Equity (Sales price minus loans)
- Sales Proceeds (Before and after taxes)
- Accumulated Earnings (wealth)

In the spreadsheet versions of REA/L, you have control over how you'd like the graphs to look. Using the chart options in Excel or 1-2-3 you can make them look however you want. Want more? Add as many as you like. **You have complete access and control over the worksheets.**

Cash Flow - End of year Sale Calculations

(table: SALE CALCULATIONS — ADJUSTED BASIS, GAIN ON SALE, SUSPENDED LOSS CARRYFORWARD, TAX LIABILITY ON SALE, SALE PROCEEDS, NET PRESENT VALUE, for years 1996–2005; figures not legible)

REA/L SOFTWARE (C)Copyright 1988-89 J. Roger Martin CCIM, Portland OR

INVESTMENT SUMMARY

Price	650,000
Total Loans	500,000
Loan to Value Ratio	76.92%
Initial Investment	150,000
Acquisition Fees	0
Total Annual Debt Service Year One	53,164
Annualized Loan Constant	10.63
Debt Coverage Ratio	1.10
Gross Rent Multiplier	6.60
Potential Total Income	100,500
Vacancy and Operating Expenses	42,100
Net Operating Income	58,400
Capitalization Rate	8.98%
N.O.I. as Percent of Potential Total Income	58.11%
Cash Flow Before Taxes, Year One	5,236
Cash on Cash Percentage, Year One	3.49%
Tax Liability at a tax rate of 31.00%	-1,938
Cash Flow After Taxes, Year One	7,174
After Tax Cash on Cash	4.78%
Internal Rate of Return, End of Year Ten	12.48%
Financial Management Rate of Return	11.96%
Accumulated Wealth at End of Year Ten	464,210

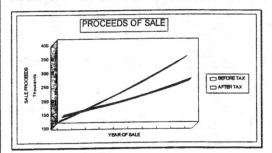
PROCEEDS OF SALE

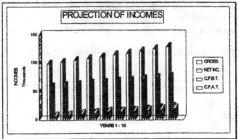
PROJECTION OF INCOMES

ROGER MARTIN COMPANY   **P. O. BOX 1148**   **TUALATIN, OR 97062-1148**

Index

Accumulated earnings, 149

ACS (Alternative Cash Sales) Worksheet
  Adjusted Basis calculation on, 64
  appreciation yield on, 68
  blank form, 59, Appendix A-3
  Capital Gain on Sale calculation on, 65
  equity build-up yield on, 68
  Excess Cost Recovery calculation on,
    64-65
  Income Stream on, 58-68
  investment variables on, 116-17, 122
  Items Taxed as Ordinary Income
    section of, 65-66
  line-by-line explanation of, 64-66
  Mortgage Balances section of, 60-61
  projected sales price on, 122
  Sales Proceeds after Tax calculation
    on, 66
  Sales Proceeds calculations on, 61-64,
    66
  sample form, 67
  summary of, 68

Advantages
  of Income Stream, ii-iv
  of real estate investment, 1-2

Alternative Cash Sales Worksheet.
  See ACS (Alternative Cash Sales)
Worksheet

Annual Property Operating Data
Worksheet.
  See APOD (Annual Property Operating
Data) Worksheet

APOD (Annual Property Operating Data)
Worksheet
  "Acquisition Costs" line of, 38
  "Adjusted Basis" line on, 38
  "Assessed/Appraised Values" section
    of, 37-38
  blank form, 32, Appendix A-1
  as Broker's Reconstruction Statement,
    34-35
  "Cash Flow Before Taxes" line of, 42,
    43
  cash yield on, 42, 43, 57, 68
  closing costs and loan points on, 119
  "Comments/Footnotes" on, 35
  "Down Payment" line of, 38
  Expenses line on, 118
  Financing section of, 38, 118-119
  "Income from Property" section of, 41
  Income Stream on, 30-43
  investment variables on, 116, 117-120
  Land to Improvement and Personal
    Property Allocation on, 119-120
  line-by-line explanation of, 37-38, 41-42
  "Loan Costs" line of, 38
  new information inserted in, 35
  "Operating Expenses" section of, 41-42
  overview of, 31-33
  as Owner's Statement, 33-34
  "Purchase Price" line of, 38
  "Purpose Line" of, 33, 36
  Rents line on, 117
  sample forms, 38-40
  side notes about, 37
  Specific Buyer's criteria on, 36
  summary of, 42-43
  temporary investment variables on,
    118-120

uses of, 33-37
Vacancy and Credit Loss line on, 118
Appraised value, 101-102, 125-127
Appreciation
definition of, 21-22
and demands of people, 22
inflation and, 22-23
upkeep and, 23-24
value appreciation as powerful, 27
Appreciation yield
on ACS Worksheet, 68
definition and description of, 21-27, 29, 48-49

Bonds, 115, 170-171
Broker's Reconstruction Statement, APOD Worksheet as, 34-35
Buildings
condition of, 158-159
depreciation of, 46
upkeep of, 23-24

Calculators, 93, 97
Caliber of credit, 11
Cap rate, 76-77
Capital gain on ACS Worksheet, 65
Capitalization rate, 76-77
Cash, definition of, 16
Cash flow analysis (computer software), Appendix B
Cash Flow Analysis Worksheet. See CFA (Cash Flow Analysis) Worksheet
Cash yield
on APOD Worksheet, 42, 43, 57, 68

definition and description of, 16, 27, 28, 48
on CFA Worksheet, 53, 57, 68
CCIM designation, 136
CFA (Cash Flow Analysis) Worksheet
blank form, 45, Appendix A-2
Cash Flow section of, 53
cash yield on, 53, 57, 68
Cost Recovery Data section of, 46-49, 121
Growth Factor, 54-55, 120
Income Stream on, 44-57
information blanks at top of, 46
investment variables on, 116, 120-122
line-by-line explanation of, 46-54
Mortgage Data section of, 46
Net Operating Income on, 50
Operating Expenses Pattern line on, 120-121
sample forms, 47, 48, 49, 51, 53, 56
summary of, 57
tax bracket of owner on, 121-122
tax shelter yield on, 52-53, 57, 68
temporary investment variables on, 121-122
Year line of, 49
CIREI. See Commercial Investment Real Estate Institute (CIREI)
Commercial Investment Real Estate Institute (CIREI), 78, 136
Computer printout for sample property, 143-146
Computers
benefit of, 140
REA/L ESTATE ANALYSIS SOFTWARE, 141-151, Appendix B

and Real Estate Investment Analysis,
133-134, 136-137
Cost recovery
    on ACS Worksheet, 64-66
    on CFA Worksheet, 46-49, 50, 121
    definition and description of, 17-18

DCF. See Discounted Cash Flow (DCF)
Debt coverage ratio, 156
Depreciation
    on ACS Worksheet, 64-66
    on CFA Worksheet, 46-49, 50
    definition and description of, 17-18
    of improvements (buildings), 46
    land not depreciable, 46
    of personal property, 46-47
Discounted Cash Flow (DCF), 78,
    79-81
Durability of Income Stream, 12-14

Earnings, accumulated, 149
Equity
    gross equity, 150
    increase in, 132-133
Equity build-up yield
    on ACS Worksheet, 68
    definition and description of, 21, 24-27,
    29, 48-49
Evaluation of real estate. See Value
    of real estate
Excess cost recovery on ACS
Worksheet, 64-66
Exchanging the property, iii-iv,
    19-21, 134, 135
Expenses
    on APOD Worksheet, 41-42, 118

on CFA Worksheet, 120-121
increase in, 131

Financial calculators, 93, 97
Financial Management Rate of
Return (FMRR), 138-140
FMRR (Financial Management Rate of
    Return), 138-140

Gold, 115, 167, 171
Greater Fool caution, 158-159
Gross equity, 150
Gross operating income, 131
Growth Factor, 54-55, 120
Growth potential, 165

Hewlett-Packard calculators, 97
Horn of Plenty, 24-26

Income, from rental property
    versus business, 6-8
Income projections, 149, Appendix B
Income Stream. See also Yield
    elements of Income Stream
    on ACS (Alternative Cash Sales)
Worksheet, 58-68
    advantages of, ii-iv
    on APOD (Annual Property Operating
    Data) Worksheet, 30-43
    on CFA (Cash Flow Analysis)
    Worksheet, 44-57
    definition of, 4
    durability of, 12-14
    for investments other than real estate,
    162-176
    length of, 12

location and, 4-5
quality of, 10-11, 13-14
quantity of, 10, 13-14
"smoke screens" concerning, 8-9
stability of, 12
test of, 9-14
valuing real estate using, 98-107
"yield elements" of, 15-29
Inflation, iii, 22-23, 155
Installment Loan Pattern, 87-93,
    96-97
Insurance annuity, 163
Interest payment, decrease in, 132
Internal Rate of Return (IRR)
    adequacy of yield, 155
    arriving at property value to suit
        personal IRR, 102-103
    calculators for, 93, 97
    compared with Financial Management
        Rate of Return (FMRR), 138-140
    compared with interest yield, 155
    definition of, 95-96
    example on, 93-94, 148
    graph on, 148
    introduction to, 77-79
    value of existing property using,
        103-105
Investment alternatives, 134-136
Investment base, 137-138, 140
Investment criteria, 164-166
Investment diversification, 165-166
Investment Pattern, compared with
    Installment Loan Pattern, 90-93, 96-97
Investment real estate.
    See Real estate investments; Value of
        real estate

Investment summary (computer
    software), 147, Appendix B
Investment variables
    on ACS Worksheet, 116-17, 122
    on APOD Worksheet, 116, 117-120
    on CFA Worksheet, 116, 120-122
    list of, 116-117
    and risk assessment, 113-114, 124,
        164-166
    Summary Sheet on, 122-123
Investments. See Income Stream; Real
    estate investments
IRR. See Internal Rate of Return (IRR)
IRS, 17, 19-20, 121
IRV Formula, 75-76

Keeping the property, 134

Land purchase, 163, 170, 171
Landlord's view of location, 5-6
Length of Income Stream, 12
Leverage, power of, 153-155
Life insurance, 172, 173-175
Liquidity, 9, 108-110, 165
Location
    importance of, 2-5
    user's (or tenant's) versus landlord's
        view of, 5-6

Management
    as investment criteria, 165
    of investment real estate, 156-161
Martin, J. Roger, 142
Mortgage as investment, 163,
    168-169, 171

Mortgage payments, 46, 60-61, 156
Municipal bonds, 170-171

NAR. See National Association of
    Realtors (NAR)
National Association of Realtors
    (NAR), 31, 78, 136
"Negative" yield, 85-86
Net Operating Income (NOI)
    debt coverage ratio and, 156
    for estimation of property value, 99-102
    on CFA Worksheet, 50
Net Present Value (NPV), 78, 81
NOI. See Net Operating Income (NOI)
NPV. See Net Present Value (NPV)

100% occupancy rate, 159-160
Operating expenses
    on APOD Worksheet, 41-42, 118
    on CFA Worksheet, 120-121
Operating statements (computer
    software), Appendix B
Over-priced property, 105-106
Owner's Statement, APOD Worksheet
    as, 33-34
Ownership of investment real
    estate, 152-161

Personal property,
    depreciation of, 46-47
Power of Leverage principle,
    153-155
Present value.
    See Net present value (NPV)
"Price Per" Index, 73-74

Proceeds of sale, 61-64, 66, 150,
    Appendix B
Projected sales price. See ACS
    (Alternative Cash Sales) Worksheet
Projection of incomes, 149, Appendix
    B
Property management, 156-161
Property values. See Value of real
    estate

Quality of Income Stream, 10-11,
    13-14
Quantity of Income Stream, 10,
    13-14

Rate of return.
    See Financial Management Rate of
        Return (FMRR); Internal Rate
        of Return (IRR)
REA/L ESTATE ANALYSIS
SOFTWARE, 141-151, Appendix B
Real estate appraisals, 101-102
Real Estate Investment Analysis,
    133-134, 136-137
Real estate investments.
    See also Income Stream; Value of real
        estate
    advantages of, 1-2
    alternatives in, 134-136
    condition of buildings and
        improvements, 159-160
    demand for rental property, 152-153
    equity increasing, 132-133
    exchanging the property, iii-iv, 19-21,
        134, 135
    expenses increasing, 131

fluctuations in yield from, 128-134
and Greater Fool caution, 158-159
gross operating income going up or
   down, 131
income from rental property, 6-8
interest payment decreasing, 132
keeping the property, 134
liquidity and, 108-110, 165
location and, 2-5
ownership and management of,
   152-161
rental property, 6-8
replacement value of, 8
risk factors in, 110-114, 124, 164-166
selling the property, 134, 135
"smoke screens" on, 8-9
tax basis decreasing, 132
value increasing, 133
value of income property as income
   production, 8, 35, 98

Rental property.
   See also Real estate investment
   demand for, 152-153
   income from, 6-8
   100% occupancy rate, 159-160
   upkeep of, 23-24

Rents line on APOD Worksheet,
   117

Replacement value, 8

Return on investment.
   See Financial Management Rate of
   Return (FMRR); Internal Rate of
   Return (IRR)

Risk, 110-114, 124, 164-166

Roger Martin Co., 141-151, Appendix
   B

Rogers, Will, 2

Rules of Thumb. See Thumb-rules

Sale proceeds calculations
   on ACS Worksheet, 61-64, 66
   with computer software, 150, Appendix
   B

Sales price. See ACS (Alternative Cash
   Sales) Worksheet

Savings accounts, 172, 173

Selling the property, 134, 135,
   160-161

"Smoke screens" on investments,
   8-9

Software for real estate analysis,
   141-151, Appendix B

Specific Buyer's criteria on APOD
   Worksheet, 36

Stability of Income stream, 12

Stocks, 115, 163, 168, 171

Summary Sheet, 122-123, Appendix
   A-4

Tax basis, decrease in, 132

Tax bracket, 121-122, 127-128

Tax consequences of investments,
   165

Tax-deferred exchange, iii-iv, 19-21,
   134, 135

Tax shelter
   definition of, 17-18
   for real estate investment, iii

Tax shelter yield
   definition and description of, 16-21, 27,
   28-29, 48
   on CFA Worksheet, 52-53, 57, 68

Tee Bar, 83-86, 88, 91, 139, 148, 167-171, 173, 175
Tenant's view of location, 5-6
Term insurance, 174-175
Test of Income Stream, 9-14
Texas Instruments calculators, 97
Thumb-rules
  background on, 70-71
  capitalization rate, 76-77
  "Cash-on-Cash" method, 74-75
  IRV Formula, 75-76
  "Price Per" Index, 73-74
  purposes of, 72-73
  weaknesses of, 71-72
Time value of money, 79-81

Upkeep and appreciation, 23-24

Vacancy and Credit Loss line on APOD Worksheet, 118
Value appreciation, 27
Value of real estate
  appraised value, 101-102, 125-127
  arriving at value to suit personal IRR, 102-103
  different value of same property for different people, 127-128
  fluctuations in yield, 128-134
  income production and, 8, 35, 98
  increase in, 133
  IRR for valuing existing property, 103-105
  need for analysis of, 106-107
  Net Operating Income (NOI) for estimation of, 99-102
  Net Present Value (NPV), 78, 81
  over-priced property, 105-106

as predicated on future use, 114-115
using Income Stream, 98-107

"Whole-life" life insurance, 172, 173-175
"Wudjatake" game, 160-161

Yield elements of Income Stream
  appreciation yield, 21-27, 29, 48-49, 68
  cash yield, 16, 27, 28, 42, 48, 53, 57, 68
  equity build-up yield, 21, 24-27, 29, 48-49, 68
  overview of, 15-16, 28-29
  tax shelter yield, 16-21, 27, 28-29, 48, 57, 68
Yield factors of investment, 165

ORDER FORM

Please send me _____ copies of the **"INCOME STREAM"**

Price Per Copy - **$22.95**   (Discounts Available For Quanity Purchase)
Please add $1.75 per copy for shipping
Plus ____% Tax if in Texas.

Mail order to:

Brookstone Publications
P.O. Box 811 Los Fresnos, TX 78566

Send Order to:

Name_____

Address_____

City_____State____Zip_____

Telephone (_____)_____

Payment: ☐Check   ☐Visa   ☐Mastercard

Card Number _____Exp. Date_____

Name on Card _____

ORDER FORM

Please send me _____ copies of the **"INCOME STREAM"**

Price Per Copy - **$22.95**   (Discounts Available For Quanity Purchase)
Please add $1.75 per copy for shipping
Plus ____% Tax if in Texas.

Mail order to:

Brookstone Publications
P.O. Box 811 Los Fresnos, TX 78566

Send Order to:

Name_____

Address_____

City_____State____Zip_____

Telephone (_____)_____

Payment: ☐Check   ☐Visa   ☐Mastercard

Card Number _____Exp. Date_____

Name on Card _____